CLARITY
scout
GUIDES FOR BETTER LIVING

Goals With Gratitude Workbook

ISBN 9781710625295

CLARITY
sc**out
GUIDES FOR BETTER LIVING

GOALS WITH GRATITUDE
WORKBOOK

Focus on Gratitude and Habits
in Order to Meet Your Goals

by Sara Wadford

INTRODUCTION

I don't claim to be an expert on goal-setting, self-help or pretty much anything. It's not in my nature to boast or brag about my accomplishments and talents. However, when it comes to anxiety, I feel like I have expert-level knowledge. I have spent the better part of my adult years with anxiety at the wheel, keeping me from enjoying down-time, everyday moments, and keeping me stagnant, thus making it difficult to move forward with large goals.

I have kept a journal for this past year, writing down three things I am grateful for each day. It has really helped me to acknowledge that living in the moment *is* possible. I have begun to appreciate the small things rather than getting tied up with all the anxious chatter in my head. For instance, the electric bill will be due every month; however, I can take a moment to be grateful that a coworker brought me flowers for my birthday. What I like best about the process is that I have had a place to write and capture the simple moments that have brought me joy each day.

The process led me to think about how I would feel about reaching and setting goals. I tend to have big ideas and little or no follow-through because of the unsurmountable tasks associated with the idea. In reality, the tasks are nothing more than a series of small to-do items and a few behavioral changes. My mind translates this into a huge list of impossible tasks – some that I don't even know how to complete, turning it into a daunting project. I became tired of this thinking and sought to find a solution that worked for me.

I began by experimenting with breaking down my own goals into smaller and manageable pieces. I kept notes of the process, but as I completed my gratitude journal each day, I began to notice how the two could be connected.

I immediately began combining the two ideas of Gratitude and Goal Setting and have put together this journal. If I have had this much trouble following through with big goals, someone else must have the same problem. I made this journal for both of us. Not only do I want this to be the place you keep your happiest moments for the next twelve months, I want this to be the place that helps you dig deep, set up, and achieve some exceptional goals that you haven't been able to sort out and accomplish. Since it has worked for me, I know that it will work for you if you open your mind and dedicate some time to the process.

JOURNALING YOUR GRATITUDE:
Nothing is too big or too small. Just strive for consistency. For example, some days you may have so many things to write down that you may wonder why I'm asking you to list just three things you're grateful for each day! Other days you may struggle to find one shining moment in your day. It's okay – it's all about the long-term picture, and recognizing the everyday things that truly make you happy.

DETERMINING YOUR GOALS:
Use the goal-building sections to brainstorm the small steps that it will take to make it to your goal. If you want to lose

weight, think of all the steps that it will take to achieve that goal. Don't freak out by the amount of items on your list. There's a time and a place for everything, and the most important thing is to START SMALL.

Don't over-think your goals; be realistic and honest with yourself. For instance, if your goal is to save money for your high school senior to enter college next year but you only have an extra fifty dollars in your budget each month, you most likely won't reach that goal within twelve months. If your goal is to find a higher-paying job, this journal can help you work toward that goal.

ABOUT THE JOURNAL:
Write in it. Take it with you. Drop it. Step on it. Love it so much that you buy yourself another copy for next year – whatever. Fill it out in the morning. Fill it out in the evening. Whatever works for *you*. I'm personally someone who does best checking in at night when I'm alone, just before I read and fall asleep. Remember, you will only stay on task if you use the journal daily.

There are no guarantees in life and this journal is no exception. It is simply meant to be a tool to help you achieve your goals. It is really your strength, determination, and tenacity that will get you what you want in life. I truly hope that this journal format helps you as much as it has helped me.

Best wishes,

Sara

STARTING SOMEWHERE:

List the possible goals you would like to achieve during the
next twelve months:

_____

_____

_____

_____

_____

*Keep in mind that you don't have to stick to one goal, and you don't
have to stay with that goal through the whole year. Life is fluid, and
things change without notice. You have to adapt to life's changes, as well
as to your goals.*

Look at your list of goals. Which is the most important to you
at this moment? _____

Which goal do you feel most passionate about? _____

_____

Which goal may be most important to those in your life? _____

_____

Which goal gives you the most happiness when you imagine
yourself making that goal? _____

Next, list your goals in order of importance based on what
you have just contemplated. Decide if the goal at the top of
your list is the **Primary Goal** you would like to work toward.

_____

_____

_____

_____

_____

I've decided that the **Primary Goal** I would like to work toward in the next twelve months is _____

UNDERSTANDING THE TERMINOLOGY:

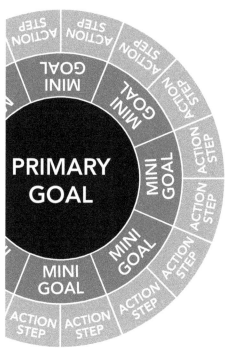

I've developed this goal-setting system so that all of the small steps are recognized and all of the big steps aren't too overwhelming. The chart on the left demonstrates the impact of **Mini Goals** and **Action Steps** throughout this process.

Primary Goal: The main project you have decided to work on over the next twelve months.

Mini Goal: **Mini Goals** are smaller components to your **Primary Goal**. **Mini Goals** may take a little work, and they may even need to develop into a habit, but with daily check-ins and weekly planning, the **Mini Goals** will add up to large achievements toward your **Primary Goal**.

Action Step: These are tasks that need to be completed in order to achieve a **Mini Goal**. Some **Action Steps** will need to be repeated to help develop an overall habit. Others are one-time tasks that can be completed so that you can move on.

Brainstorm what steps you need to complete in order to achieve your goal. Be very specific. No step is too small. You may find that you don't have to spend a lot of time focusing on each step becoming a habit. Sometimes they are simply tasks needing completion. Whether they are long-term habits or short and quick tasks, list them here:

_____   _____
_____   _____
_____   _____
_____   _____
_____   _____
_____   _____
_____   _____
_____   _____
_____   _____
_____   _____
_____   _____
_____   _____
_____   _____
_____   _____
_____   _____
_____   _____
_____   _____
_____   _____
_____   _____

_____   _____

_____   _____

_____   _____

_____   _____

_____   _____

_____   _____

_____   _____

_____   _____

_____   _____

_____   _____

_____   _____

_____   _____

_____   _____

_____   _____

_____   _____

_____   _____

_____   _____

_____   _____

_____   _____

_____   _____

_____   _____

Review the steps you've listed. Do any of these steps need multiple actions to complete? If so, mark them with a star and go to the next step on the following page.

DEFINING MINI GOALS & ACTION STEPS:

List each step from the previous list that you drew a star next to on the lines that begin with a " ★ " below. We will call these **Mini Goals** from here on out. This is where you will break down the step into smaller **Action Steps**. List each small **Action Step** that you will need to do in order to complete the **Mini Goal** listed below. *If you are trying for a clean house, each starred item* **Mini Goal** *could be a certain room you would need to clean, and the small arrow (↳) lines would be the* **Action Steps** *within each room to complete.*

★   <u>Clean kitchen</u>   ★   _____

   ↳   <u>Wash dishes</u>   ↳ _____

   ↳   <u>Scrub stove top</u>   ↳ _____

   ↳   <u>Clean counters</u>   ↳ _____

   ↳   <u>Wash floor</u>   ↳ _____

★ _____   ★ _____

   ↳ _____   ↳ _____

   ↳ _____   ↳ _____

   ↳ _____   ↳ _____

   ↳ _____   ↳ _____

★ _____   ★ _____

   ↳ _____   ↳ _____

   ↳ _____   ↳ _____

   ↳ _____   ↳ _____

   ↳ _____   ↳ _____

★ _____

  ↳ _____

  ↳ _____

  ↳ _____

  ↳ _____

★ _____

  ↳ _____

  ↳ _____

  ↳ _____

  ↳ _____

★ _____

  ↳ _____

  ↳ _____

  ↳ _____

  ↳ _____

★ _____

  ↳ _____

  ↳ _____

  ↳ _____

  ↳ _____

★ _____

  ↳ _____

  ↳ _____

  ↳ _____

  ↳ _____

★ _____

  ↳ _____

  ↳ _____

  ↳ _____

  ↳ _____

★ _____

  ↳ _____

  ↳ _____

  ↳ _____

  ↳ _____

★ _____

  ↳ _____

  ↳ _____

  ↳ _____

  ↳ _____

★ _____

  ↳ _____

  ↳ _____

  ↳ _____

  ↳ _____

★ _____

  ↳ _____

  ↳ _____

  ↳ _____

  ↳ _____

★ _____
  ↳ _____
  ↳ _____
  ↳ _____
  ↳ _____

★ _____
  ↳ _____
  ↳ _____
  ↳ _____
  ↳ _____

★ _____
  ↳ _____
  ↳ _____
  ↳ _____
  ↳ _____

★ _____
  ↳ _____
  ↳ _____
  ↳ _____
  ↳ _____

★ _____
  ↳ _____
  ↳ _____
  ↳ _____
  ↳ _____

★ _____
  ↳ _____
  ↳ _____
  ↳ _____
  ↳ _____

★ _____
  ↳ _____
  ↳ _____
  ↳ _____
  ↳ _____

★ _____
  ↳ _____
  ↳ _____
  ↳ _____
  ↳ _____

★ _____
  ↳ _____
  ↳ _____
  ↳ _____
  ↳ _____

★ _____
  ↳ _____
  ↳ _____
  ↳ _____
  ↳ _____

★ _____   ★ _____
  ↳ _____   ↳ _____
  ↳ _____   ↳ _____
  ↳ _____   ↳ _____
  ↳ _____   ↳ _____

★ _____   ★ _____
  ↳ _____   ↳ _____
  ↳ _____   ↳ _____
  ↳ _____   ↳ _____
  ↳ _____   ↳ _____

★ _____   ★ _____
  ↳ _____   ↳ _____
  ↳ _____   ↳ _____
  ↳ _____   ↳ _____
  ↳ _____   ↳ _____

★ _____   ★ _____
  ↳ _____   ↳ _____
  ↳ _____   ↳ _____
  ↳ _____   ↳ _____
  ↳ _____   ↳ _____

Look through the list once more and notice those items that will need to become habits in order to achieve success. Mark those items with an "H" and give them extra attention and time when planning your weekly and daily goals. A habit can be an **Action Step** or even a **Mini Goal** – but a habit will take longer to become part of your daily life. It's okay if you spend a few weeks forming one habit by repeating the same **Action Step**.

ADDITIONAL **ACTION STEPS**:

Additional **Action Steps** are simple things that you can do to get you closer to your goal but that don't really require everyday practice. *If running a marathon is your* **Primary Goal**, *an* **Action Step** *could be choosing which marathon you would like to participate in. This isn't something you need to work on everyday, yet it is essential to reaching your goal.* Slot these items into easy, medium, and hard categories. Tick them off as you complete each item, and make sure that you look back to this page often to see any progress that you have made. This section is also helpful when planning your weekly goals. Remember that every small step leads to the ultimate goal.

EASY:

❏	_____	❏	_____
❏	_____	❏	_____
❏	_____	❏	_____
❏	_____	❏	_____
❏	_____	❏	_____
❏	_____	❏	_____
❏	_____	❏	_____
❏	_____	❏	_____
❏	_____	❏	_____
❏	_____	❏	_____
❏	_____	❏	_____
❏	_____	❏	_____

MEDIUM:

❏ _____
❏ _____
❏ _____
❏ _____
❏ _____
❏ _____
❏ _____
❏ _____
❏ _____
❏ _____
❏ _____
❏ _____
❏ _____
❏ _____
❏ _____
❏ _____
❏ _____
❏ _____
❏ _____
❏ _____
❏ _____
❏ _____
❏ _____
❏ _____

HARD:

❏ _____
❏ _____
❏ _____
❏ _____
❏ _____
❏ _____
❏ _____
❏ _____
❏ _____
❏ _____
❏ _____
❏ _____
❏ _____
❏ _____
❏ _____
❏ _____
❏ _____
❏ _____
❏ _____
❏ _____
❏ _____
❏ _____
❏ _____
❏ _____

NEWLY FORMED HABITS:

Habits are not easy to form. They take time, patience, and extra care to put in place. Recognize your newly formed habits on the lines below. Be sure to write them down on the lines below. If you find yourself frustrated, this is the first page to turn to and view your most difficult accomplishments during the process.

OTHER ACCOMPLISHMENTS:

Give yourself some high fives! List anything that you would like to recognize as an accomplishment during your journey. It doesn't even have to be an **Action Step** or a **Mini Goal**.

_____   _____

_____   _____

_____   _____

_____   _____

_____   _____

_____   _____

_____   _____

_____   _____

_____   _____

_____   _____

_____   _____

_____   _____

_____   _____

_____   _____

_____   _____

_____   _____

_____   _____

_____   _____

_____   _____

FRAME YOUR FIRST WEEK:

My **Primary Goal** is: _____

_____

What **Mini Goal** would you like to work on this week?

_____

Why is this **Mini Goal** important in your goal process? _____

_____

The habit I would like to focus on this week is: _____

_____

Action Steps I can do to work toward my goal this week are:

_____ _____

_____ _____

_____ _____

_____ _____

*Plan out and list your **Action Steps** and habit goals on the line for each day; as you complete these tasks, check them off!*
Each day list three things that make you feel grateful.

MONTH / DAY	1 _____
	2 _____
	3 _____

Action Step _____ Complete ❏
Habit goal _____ Complete ❏

MONTH / DAY	1 _____
	2 _____
	3 _____

Action Step _____ Complete ❏
Habit goal _____ Complete ❏

MONTH / DAY	1 _____
	2 _____
	3 _____

Action Step _____ Complete ❑
Habit goal _____ Complete ❑

MONTH / DAY	1 _____
	2 _____
	3 _____

Action Step _____ Complete ❑
Habit goal _____ Complete ❑

MONTH / DAY	1 _____
	2 _____
	3 _____

Action Step _____ Complete ❑
Habit goal _____ Complete ❑

MONTH / DAY	1 _____
	2 _____
	3 _____

Action Step _____ Complete ❑
Habit goal _____ Complete ❑

MONTH / DAY	1 _____
	2 _____
	3 _____

Action Step _____ Complete ❑
Habit goal _____ Complete ❑

WEEKLY RECAP – GOALS:

Did you meet your **Mini Goal** for this week? ❏ Yes ❏ No

If no, do you need to spend another week on this **Mini Goal** or would you prefer to move onto a new **Mini Goal** and return to this **Mini Goal** another time? ❏ Same ❏ New

If you answered "Yes," which goal would you like to work on this week?_____

What **Action Steps** helped the most toward achieving your goal? _____

_____

Do you need to repeat any **Action Steps** to develop a habit?

_____

What did you notice and learn?_____

WEEKLY RECAP – GRATITUDE:

Without looking back at what you have written down during the past week, answer the following questions:

What was the best part of your week?_____

_____

Who did you enjoy spending time with this week? _____

_____

Now look back at what you have written for the last week.

What do you notice about how you feel today versus how you felt in the moment? _____

_____

Did any of these moments contribute to your **Primary Goal**? If so, how? _____

_____

WEEKLY GOAL SETTING:

Refer to the previous page when completing this section.

If you did not meet your **Mini Goal**, what obstacles prevented you from doing so? _____

_____

_____

What **Action Steps** helped the most with your goal? Why?____

_____

_____

Do you need to repeat any **Action Steps** to help develop a habit? Which ones? _____

_____

What did you notice and learn?_____

_____

_____

My **Primary Goal** is: _____

The **Mini Goal** that I will work on this week is: _____

_____

Why is this **Mini Goal** important to your goal process?_____

_____

The habit that I would like to focus on to support my goal this week is: _____

Action Steps that I can do to work toward my goal this week are:

_____   _____

_____   _____

_____   _____

Plan out and list your **Action Steps** *and habit goals on the line for each day on the following page. As you complete these tasks, check them off!*

NEW WEEK + NEW FOCUS = NEW YOU:

My **Primary Goal** is: _____

It is important that I reach this goal because: _____

_____

_____

Each day list three things that make you feel grateful.

MONTH / DAY	1 _____
	2 _____
	3 _____

Action Step _____ Complete ❏

Habit goal _____ Complete ❏

Notes _____

MONTH / DAY	1 _____
	2 _____
	3 _____

Action Step _____ Complete ❏

Habit goal _____ Complete ❏

Notes _____

MONTH / DAY	1 _____
	2 _____
	3 _____

Action Step _____ Complete ❏

Habit goal _____ Complete ❏

Notes _____

MONTH / DAY	1 _____
	2 _____
	3 _____

Action Step _____ Complete ❑

Habit goal _____ Complete ❑

Notes _____

MONTH / DAY	1 _____
	2 _____
	3 _____

Action Step _____ Complete ❑

Habit goal _____ Complete ❑

Notes _____

MONTH / DAY	1 _____
	2 _____
	3 _____

Action Step _____ Complete ❑

Habit goal _____ Complete ❑

Notes _____

MONTH / DAY	1 _____
	2 _____
	3 _____

Action Step _____ Complete ❑

Habit goal _____ Complete ❑

Notes _____

WEEKLY RECAP – GOALS:

Did you meet your **Mini Goal** for this week? ❑ Yes ❑ No

If no, do you need to spend another week on this **Mini Goal** or would you prefer to move onto a new **Mini Goal** and return to this **Mini Goal** another time? ❑ Same ❑ New

If you answered "Yes," which goal would you like to work on this week?_____

What **Action Steps** helped the most toward achieving your goal? _____

_____

Do you need to repeat any **Action Steps** to develop a habit?

_____

What did you notice and learn?_____

WEEKLY RECAP – GRATITUDE:

Without looking back at what you have written down during the past week, answer the following questions:

What was the best part of your week?_____

_____

Who did you enjoy spending time with this week? _____

_____

Now look back at what you have written for the last week. What do you notice about how you feel today versus how you felt in the moment? _____

_____

Did any of these moments contribute to your **Primary Goal**? If so, how? _____

_____

WEEKLY GOAL SETTING:

Refer to the previous page when completing this section.

If you did not meet your **Mini Goal**, what obstacles prevented you from doing so? _____

_____

_____

What **Action Steps** helped the most with your goal? Why?____

_____

_____

Do you need to repeat any **Action Steps** to help develop a habit? Which ones? _____

_____

What did you notice and learn?_____

_____

_____

My **Primary Goal** is: _____

The **Mini Goal** that I will work on this week is: _____

_____

Why is this **Mini Goal** important to your goal process?_____

_____

The habit that I would like to focus on to support my goal this week is: _____

Action Steps that I can do to work toward my goal this week are:

_____   _____

_____   _____

_____   _____

*Plan out and list your **Action Steps** and habit goals on the line for each day on the following page. As you complete these tasks, check them off!*

NEW WEEK + NEW FOCUS = NEW YOU:

My **Primary Goal** is: _____

It is important that I reach this goal because: _____

_____

_____

Each day list three things that make you feel grateful.

MONTH / DAY		

1 _____

2 _____

3 _____

Action Step _____ Complete ❏

Habit goal _____ Complete ❏

Notes _____

MONTH / DAY		

1 _____

2 _____

3 _____

Action Step _____ Complete ❏

Habit goal _____ Complete ❏

Notes _____

MONTH / DAY		

1 _____

2 _____

3 _____

Action Step _____ Complete ❏

Habit goal _____ Complete ❏

Notes _____

MONTH / DAY	1 _____
	2 _____
	3 _____

Action Step _____ Complete ❏

Habit goal _____ Complete ❏

Notes _____

MONTH / DAY	1 _____
	2 _____
	3 _____

Action Step _____ Complete ❏

Habit goal _____ Complete ❏

Notes _____

MONTH / DAY	1 _____
	2 _____
	3 _____

Action Step _____ Complete ❏

Habit goal _____ Complete ❏

Notes _____

MONTH / DAY	1 _____
	2 _____
	3 _____

Action Step _____ Complete ❏

Habit goal _____ Complete ❏

Notes _____

WEEKLY RECAP – GOALS:

Did you meet your **Mini Goal** for this week? ❏ Yes ❏ No
If no, do you need to spend another week on this **Mini Goal**
or would you prefer to move onto a new **Mini Goal** and return
to this **Mini Goal** another time? ❏ Same ❏ New
If you answered "Yes," which goal would you like to work on
this week?_____
What **Action Steps** helped the most toward achieving your
goal? _____

_____

Do you need to repeat any **Action Steps** to develop a habit?

_____

What did you notice and learn?_____

WEEKLY RECAP – GRATITUDE:

Without looking back at what you have written down during
the past week, answer the following questions:
What was the best part of your week?_____

_____

Who did you enjoy spending time with this week? _____

_____

Now look back at what you have written for the last week.
What do you notice about how you feel today versus how you
felt in the moment? _____

_____

Did any of these moments contribute to your **Primary Goal**? If
so, how? _____

_____

WEEKLY GOAL SETTING:

Refer to the previous page when completing this section.

If you did not meet your **Mini Goal**, what obstacles prevented you from doing so? _____

_____

_____

What **Action Steps** helped the most with your goal? Why?____

_____

_____

Do you need to repeat any **Action Steps** to help develop a habit? Which ones? _____

_____

What did you notice and learn?_____

_____

_____

My **Primary Goal** is: _____

The **Mini Goal** that I will work on this week is: _____

_____

Why is this **Mini Goal** important to your goal process?_____

_____

The habit that I would like to focus on to support my goal this week is: _____

Action Steps that I can do to work toward my goal this week are:

_____   _____

_____   _____

_____   _____

Plan out and list your **Action Steps** *and habit goals on the line for each day on the following page. As you complete these tasks, check them off!*

NEW WEEK + NEW FOCUS = NEW YOU:

My **Primary Goal** is: _____

It is important that I reach this goal because: _____

_____

_____

Each day list three things that make you feel grateful.

MONTH / DAY	1 _____
	2 _____
	3 _____

Action Step _____ Complete ❑

Habit goal _____ Complete ❑

Notes _____

MONTH / DAY	1 _____
	2 _____
	3 _____

Action Step _____ Complete ❑

Habit goal _____ Complete ❑

Notes _____

MONTH / DAY	1 _____
	2 _____
	3 _____

Action Step _____ Complete ❑

Habit goal _____ Complete ❑

Notes _____

```
MONTH        1 _____
             2 _____
        DAY  3 _____
```

Action Step _____ Complete ❑

Habit goal   _____ Complete ❑

Notes   _____

```
MONTH        1 _____
             2 _____
        DAY  3 _____
```

Action Step _____ Complete ❑

Habit goal   _____ Complete ❑

Notes   _____

```
MONTH        1 _____
             2 _____
        DAY  3 _____
```

Action Step _____ Complete ❑

Habit goal   _____ Complete ❑

Notes   _____

```
MONTH        1 _____
             2 _____
        DAY  3 _____
```

Action Step _____ Complete ❑

Habit goal   _____ Complete ❑

Notes   _____

WEEKLY RECAP – GOALS:

Did you meet your **Mini Goal** for this week? ❑ Yes ❑ No
If no, do you need to spend another week on this **Mini Goal**
or would you prefer to move onto a new **Mini Goal** and return
to this **Mini Goal** another time? ❑ Same ❑ New
If you answered "Yes," which goal would you like to work on
this week?_____
What **Action Steps** helped the most toward achieving your
goal? _____
_____

Do you need to repeat any **Action Steps** to develop a habit?
_____

What did you notice and learn?_____

WEEKLY RECAP – GRATITUDE:

Without looking back at what you have written down during
the past week, answer the following questions:
What was the best part of your week? _____
_____

Who did you enjoy spending time with this week? _____
_____

Now look back at what you have written for the last week.
What do you notice about how you feel today versus how you
felt in the moment? _____
_____

Did any of these moments contribute to your **Primary Goal**? If
so, how? _____
_____

WEEKLY GOAL SETTING:

Refer to the previous page when completing this section.

If you did not meet your **Mini Goal**, what obstacles prevented you from doing so? _____

_____

_____

What **Action Steps** helped the most with your goal? Why?____

_____

_____

Do you need to repeat any **Action Steps** to help develop a habit? Which ones? _____

_____

What did you notice and learn?_____

_____

_____

My **Primary Goal** is: _____

The **Mini Goal** that I will work on this week is: _____

_____

Why is this **Mini Goal** important to your goal process?_____

_____

The habit that I would like to focus on to support my goal this week is: _____

Action Steps that I can do to work toward my goal this week are:

_____   _____

_____   _____

_____   _____

*Plan out and list your **Action Steps** and habit goals on the line for each day on the following page. As you complete these tasks, check them off!*

NEW WEEK + NEW FOCUS = NEW YOU:

My **Primary Goal** is: _____

It is important that I reach this goal because: _____

_____

_____

Each day list three things that make you feel grateful.

MONTH / DAY	1 _____
	2 _____
	3 _____

Action Step _____ Complete ❏

Habit goal _____ Complete ❏

Notes _____

MONTH / DAY	1 _____
	2 _____
	3 _____

Action Step _____ Complete ❏

Habit goal _____ Complete ❏

Notes _____

MONTH / DAY	1 _____
	2 _____
	3 _____

Action Step _____ Complete ❏

Habit goal _____ Complete ❏

Notes _____

```
┌─────────┐
│ MONTH  ╱│   1 _____
│       ╱ │   2 _____
│      ╱  │   3 _____
│    ╱ DAY│
└─────────┘
```

Action Step _____ Complete ❑

Habit goal _____ Complete ❑

Notes _____

```
┌─────────┐
│ MONTH  ╱│   1 _____
│       ╱ │   2 _____
│      ╱  │   3 _____
│    ╱ DAY│
└─────────┘
```

Action Step _____ Complete ❑

Habit goal _____ Complete ❑

Notes _____

```
┌─────────┐
│ MONTH  ╱│   1 _____
│       ╱ │   2 _____
│      ╱  │   3 _____
│    ╱ DAY│
└─────────┘
```

Action Step _____ Complete ❑

Habit goal _____ Complete ❑

Notes _____

```
┌─────────┐
│ MONTH  ╱│   1 _____
│       ╱ │   2 _____
│      ╱  │   3 _____
│    ╱ DAY│
└─────────┘
```

Action Step _____ Complete ❑

Habit goal _____ Complete ❑

Notes _____

WEEKLY RECAP – GOALS:

Did you meet your **Mini Goal** for this week? ❏ Yes ❏ No

If no, do you need to spend another week on this **Mini Goal** or would you prefer to move onto a new **Mini Goal** and return to this **Mini Goal** another time? ❏ Same ❏ New

If you answered "Yes," which goal would you like to work on this week?_____

What **Action Steps** helped the most toward achieving your goal? _____

_____

Do you need to repeat any **Action Steps** to develop a habit?

_____

What did you notice and learn?_____

WEEKLY RECAP – GRATITUDE:

Without looking back at what you have written down during the past week, answer the following questions:

What was the best part of your week? _____

_____

Who did you enjoy spending time with this week? _____

_____

Now look back at what you have written for the last week. What do you notice about how you feel today versus how you felt in the moment? _____

_____

Did any of these moments contribute to your **Primary Goal**? If so, how? _____

_____

WEEKLY GOAL SETTING:

Refer to the previous page when completing this section.

If you did not meet your **Mini Goal**, what obstacles prevented you from doing so? _____

_____

_____

What **Action Steps** helped the most with your goal? Why?____

_____

_____

Do you need to repeat any **Action Steps** to help develop a habit? Which ones? _____

_____

What did you notice and learn? _____

_____

_____

My **Primary Goal** is: _____

The **Mini Goal** that I will work on this week is: _____

_____

Why is this **Mini Goal** important to your goal process? _____

_____

The habit that I would like to focus on to support my goal this week is: _____

Action Steps that I can do to work toward my goal this week are:

_____   _____

_____   _____

_____   _____

*Plan out and list your **Action Steps** and habit goals on the line for each day on the following page. As you complete these tasks, check them off!*

NEW WEEK + NEW FOCUS = NEW YOU:

My **Primary Goal** is: _____

It is important that I reach this goal because: _____

_____

_____

Each day list three things that make you feel grateful.

MONTH / DAY	1 _____
	2 _____
	3 _____

Action Step _____ Complete ❏

Habit goal _____ Complete ❏

Notes _____

MONTH / DAY	1 _____
	2 _____
	3 _____

Action Step _____ Complete ❏

Habit goal _____ Complete ❏

Notes _____

MONTH / DAY	1 _____
	2 _____
	3 _____

Action Step _____ Complete ❏

Habit goal _____ Complete ❏

Notes _____

```
┌─────────┐
│ MONTH ╱ │   1 _____
│      ╱  │   2 _____
│    ╱    │   3 _____
│  ╱  DAY │
└─────────┘
```

Action Step _____ Complete ❑

Habit goal _____ Complete ❑

Notes _____

```
┌─────────┐
│ MONTH ╱ │   1 _____
│      ╱  │   2 _____
│    ╱    │   3 _____
│  ╱  DAY │
└─────────┘
```

Action Step _____ Complete ❑

Habit goal _____ Complete ❑

Notes _____

```
┌─────────┐
│ MONTH ╱ │   1 _____
│      ╱  │   2 _____
│    ╱    │   3 _____
│  ╱  DAY │
└─────────┘
```

Action Step _____ Complete ❑

Habit goal _____ Complete ❑

Notes _____

```
┌─────────┐
│ MONTH ╱ │   1 _____
│      ╱  │   2 _____
│    ╱    │   3 _____
│  ╱  DAY │
└─────────┘
```

Action Step _____ Complete ❑

Habit goal _____ Complete ❑

Notes _____

WEEKLY RECAP – GOALS:

Did you meet your **Mini Goal** for this week? ❏ Yes ❏ No
If no, do you need to spend another week on this **Mini Goal**
or would you prefer to move onto a new **Mini Goal** and return
to this **Mini Goal** another time? ❏ Same ❏ New
If you answered "Yes," which goal would you like to work on
this week?_____
What **Action Steps** helped the most toward achieving your
goal? _____
_____
Do you need to repeat any **Action Steps** to develop a habit?
_____
What did you notice and learn?_____

WEEKLY RECAP – GRATITUDE:

Without looking back at what you have written down during
the past week, answer the following questions:
What was the best part of your week?_____
_____
Who did you enjoy spending time with this week? _____
_____
Now look back at what you have written for the last week.
What do you notice about how you feel today versus how you
felt in the moment? _____
_____
Did any of these moments contribute to your **Primary Goal**? If
so, how? _____
_____

WEEKLY GOAL SETTING:

Refer to the previous page when completing this section.

If you did not meet your **Mini Goal**, what obstacles prevented you from doing so? _____

_____

_____

What **Action Steps** helped the most with your goal? Why?____

_____

_____

Do you need to repeat any **Action Steps** to help develop a habit? Which ones? _____

_____

What did you notice and learn?_____

_____

_____

My **Primary Goal** is: _____

The **Mini Goal** that I will work on this week is: _____

_____

Why is this **Mini Goal** important to your goal process?_____

_____

The habit that I would like to focus on to support my goal this week is: _____

Action Steps that I can do to work toward my goal this week are:

_____   _____

_____   _____

_____   _____

Plan out and list your **Action Steps** *and habit goals on the line for each day on the following page. As you complete these tasks, check them off!*

NEW WEEK + NEW FOCUS = NEW YOU:

My **Primary Goal** is: _____

It is important that I reach this goal because: _____

_____

_____

Each day list three things that make you feel grateful.

MONTH / DAY	1 _____
	2 _____
	3 _____

Action Step _____ Complete ❑

Habit goal _____ Complete ❑

Notes _____

MONTH / DAY	1 _____
	2 _____
	3 _____

Action Step _____ Complete ❑

Habit goal _____ Complete ❑

Notes _____

MONTH / DAY	1 _____
	2 _____
	3 _____

Action Step _____ Complete ❑

Habit goal _____ Complete ❑

Notes _____

MONTH / DAY	1 _____
	2 _____
	3 _____

Action Step _____ Complete ❏

Habit goal _____ Complete ❏

Notes _____

MONTH / DAY	1 _____
	2 _____
	3 _____

Action Step _____ Complete ❏

Habit goal _____ Complete ❏

Notes _____

MONTH / DAY	1 _____
	2 _____
	3 _____

Action Step _____ Complete ❏

Habit goal _____ Complete ❏

Notes _____

MONTH / DAY	1 _____
	2 _____
	3 _____

Action Step _____ Complete ❏

Habit goal _____ Complete ❏

Notes _____

WEEKLY RECAP – GOALS:

Did you meet your **Mini Goal** for this week? ❏ Yes ❏ No

If no, do you need to spend another week on this **Mini Goal** or would you prefer to move onto a new **Mini Goal** and return to this **Mini Goal** another time? ❏ Same ❏ New

If you answered "Yes," which goal would you like to work on this week?_____

What **Action Steps** helped the most toward achieving your goal? _____

_____

Do you need to repeat any **Action Steps** to develop a habit?

_____

What did you notice and learn?_____

WEEKLY RECAP – GRATITUDE:

Without looking back at what you have written down during the past week, answer the following questions:

What was the best part of your week?_____

_____

Who did you enjoy spending time with this week? _____

_____

Now look back at what you have written for the last week.

What do you notice about how you feel today versus how you felt in the moment? _____

_____

Did any of these moments contribute to your **Primary Goal**? If so, how? _____

_____

WEEKLY GOAL SETTING:

Refer to the previous page when completing this section.

If you did not meet your **Mini Goal**, what obstacles prevented you from doing so? _____

_____

_____

What **Action Steps** helped the most with your goal? Why?____

_____

_____

Do you need to repeat any **Action Steps** to help develop a habit? Which ones? _____

_____

What did you notice and learn?_____

_____

_____

My **Primary Goal** is: _____

The **Mini Goal** that I will work on this week is: _____

_____

Why is this **Mini Goal** important to your goal process?_____

_____

The habit that I would like to focus on to support my goal this week is: _____

Action Steps that I can do to work toward my goal this week are:

_____   _____

_____   _____

_____   _____

Plan out and list your **Action Steps** *and habit goals on the line for each day on the following page. As you complete these tasks, check them off!*

NEW WEEK + NEW FOCUS = NEW YOU:

My **Primary Goal** is: _____

It is important that I reach this goal because: _____

_____

_____

Each day list three things that make you feel grateful.

MONTH / DAY	1 _____
	2 _____
	3 _____

Action Step _____ Complete ❏

Habit goal _____ Complete ❏

Notes _____

MONTH / DAY	1 _____
	2 _____
	3 _____

Action Step _____ Complete ❏

Habit goal _____ Complete ❏

Notes _____

MONTH / DAY	1 _____
	2 _____
	3 _____

Action Step _____ Complete ❏

Habit goal _____ Complete ❏

Notes _____

```
┌─────────┐
│ MONTH  ╱│  1 _____
│       ╱ │  2 _____
│     ╱   │  3 _____
│  ╱  DAY │
└─────────┘
```

Action Step _____ Complete ❏

Habit goal _____ Complete ❏

Notes _____

```
┌─────────┐
│ MONTH  ╱│  1 _____
│       ╱ │  2 _____
│     ╱   │  3 _____
│  ╱  DAY │
└─────────┘
```

Action Step _____ Complete ❏

Habit goal _____ Complete ❏

Notes _____

```
┌─────────┐
│ MONTH  ╱│  1 _____
│       ╱ │  2 _____
│     ╱   │  3 _____
│  ╱  DAY │
└─────────┘
```

Action Step _____ Complete ❏

Habit goal _____ Complete ❏

Notes _____

```
┌─────────┐
│ MONTH  ╱│  1 _____
│       ╱ │  2 _____
│     ╱   │  3 _____
│  ╱  DAY │
└─────────┘
```

Action Step _____ Complete ❏

Habit goal _____ Complete ❏

Notes _____

WEEKLY RECAP – GOALS:

Did you meet your **Mini Goal** for this week? ❏ Yes ❏ No

If no, do you need to spend another week on this **Mini Goal** or would you prefer to move onto a new **Mini Goal** and return to this **Mini Goal** another time? ❏ Same ❏ New

If you answered "Yes," which goal would you like to work on this week?_____

What **Action Steps** helped the most toward achieving your goal? _____

_____

Do you need to repeat any **Action Steps** to develop a habit?

_____

What did you notice and learn?_____

_____

WEEKLY RECAP – GRATITUDE:

Without looking back at what you have written down during the past week, answer the following questions:

What was the best part of your week?_____

_____

Who did you enjoy spending time with this week? _____

_____

Now look back at what you have written for the last week. What do you notice about how you feel today versus how you felt in the moment? _____

_____

Did any of these moments contribute to your **Primary Goal**? If so, how? _____

_____

WEEKLY GOAL SETTING:

Refer to the previous page when completing this section.

If you did not meet your **Mini Goal**, what obstacles prevented you from doing so? _____

_____

_____

What **Action Steps** helped the most with your goal? Why?____

_____

_____

Do you need to repeat any **Action Steps** to help develop a habit? Which ones? _____

_____

What did you notice and learn?_____

_____

_____

My **Primary Goal** is: _____

The **Mini Goal** that I will work on this week is: _____

_____

Why is this **Mini Goal** important to your goal process?_____

_____

The habit that I would like to focus on to support my goal this week is: _____

Action Steps that I can do to work toward my goal this week are:

_____   _____

_____   _____

_____   _____

Plan out and list your **Action Steps** *and habit goals on the line for each day on the following page. As you complete these tasks, check them off!*

NEW WEEK + NEW FOCUS = NEW YOU:

My **Primary Goal** is: _____

It is important that I reach this goal because: _____

_____

_____

Each day list three things that make you feel grateful.

MONTH / DAY	1 _____
	2 _____
	3 _____

Action Step _____ Complete ❑

Habit goal _____ Complete ❑

Notes _____

MONTH / DAY	1 _____
	2 _____
	3 _____

Action Step _____ Complete ❑

Habit goal _____ Complete ❑

Notes _____

MONTH / DAY	1 _____
	2 _____
	3 _____

Action Step _____ Complete ❑

Habit goal _____ Complete ❑

Notes _____

MONTH / DAY

1 _____
2 _____
3 _____

Action Step _____ Complete ❏
Habit goal _____ Complete ❏
Notes _____

MONTH / DAY

1 _____
2 _____
3 _____

Action Step _____ Complete ❏
Habit goal _____ Complete ❏
Notes _____

MONTH / DAY

1 _____
2 _____
3 _____

Action Step _____ Complete ❏
Habit goal _____ Complete ❏
Notes _____

MONTH / DAY

1 _____
2 _____
3 _____

Action Step _____ Complete ❏
Habit goal _____ Complete ❏
Notes _____

WEEKLY RECAP – GOALS:

Did you meet your **Mini Goal** for this week? ❑ Yes ❑ No
If no, do you need to spend another week on this **Mini Goal**
or would you prefer to move onto a new **Mini Goal** and return
to this **Mini Goal** another time? ❑ Same ❑ New
If you answered "Yes," which goal would you like to work on
this week?_____
What **Action Steps** helped the most toward achieving your
goal? _____

_____

Do you need to repeat any **Action Steps** to develop a habit?

_____

What did you notice and learn?_____

_____

WEEKLY RECAP – GRATITUDE:

Without looking back at what you have written down during
the past week, answer the following questions:
What was the best part of your week?_____

_____

Who did you enjoy spending time with this week? _____

_____

Now look back at what you have written for the last week.
What do you notice about how you feel today versus how you
felt in the moment? _____

_____

Did any of these moments contribute to your **Primary Goal**? If
so, how? _____

_____

WEEKLY GOAL SETTING:

Refer to the previous page when completing this section.
If you did not meet your **Mini Goal**, what obstacles prevented you from doing so? _____

_____

_____

What **Action Steps** helped the most with your goal? Why?____

_____

_____

Do you need to repeat any **Action Steps** to help develop a habit? Which ones? _____

_____

What did you notice and learn?_____

_____

_____

My **Primary Goal** is: _____

The **Mini Goal** that I will work on this week is: _____

_____

Why is this **Mini Goal** important to your goal process?_____

_____

The habit that I would like to focus on to support my goal this week is: _____

Action Steps that I can do to work toward my goal this week are:

_____   _____

_____   _____

_____   _____

*Plan out and list your **Action Steps** and habit goals on the line for each day on the following page. As you complete these tasks, check them off!*

NEW WEEK + NEW FOCUS = NEW YOU:

My **Primary Goal** is: _____

It is important that I reach this goal because: _____

_____

_____

Each day list three things that make you feel grateful.

MONTH / DAY	1 _____
	2 _____
	3 _____

Action Step _____ Complete ❏

Habit goal _____ Complete ❏

Notes _____

MONTH / DAY	1 _____
	2 _____
	3 _____

Action Step _____ Complete ❏

Habit goal _____ Complete ❏

Notes _____

MONTH / DAY	1 _____
	2 _____
	3 _____

Action Step _____ Complete ❏

Habit goal _____ Complete ❏

Notes _____

MONTH / DAY

1 _____
2 _____
3 _____

Action Step _____ Complete ❑

Habit goal _____ Complete ❑

Notes _____

MONTH / DAY

1 _____
2 _____
3 _____

Action Step _____ Complete ❑

Habit goal _____ Complete ❑

Notes _____

MONTH / DAY

1 _____
2 _____
3 _____

Action Step _____ Complete ❑

Habit goal _____ Complete ❑

Notes _____

MONTH / DAY

1 _____
2 _____
3 _____

Action Step _____ Complete ❑

Habit goal _____ Complete ❑

Notes _____

WEEKLY RECAP – GOALS:

Did you meet your **Mini Goal** for this week? ❑ Yes ❑ No
If no, do you need to spend another week on this **Mini Goal**
or would you prefer to move onto a new **Mini Goal** and return
to this **Mini Goal** another time? ❑ Same ❑ New
If you answered "Yes," which goal would you like to work on
this week?_____
What **Action Steps** helped the most toward achieving your
goal? _____
_____
Do you need to repeat any **Action Steps** to develop a habit?
_____
What did you notice and learn?_____
_____

WEEKLY RECAP – GRATITUDE:

Without looking back at what you have written down during
the past week, answer the following questions:
What was the best part of your week? _____
_____
Who did you enjoy spending time with this week? _____
_____
Now look back at what you have written for the last week.
What do you notice about how you feel today versus how you
felt in the moment? _____
_____
Did any of these moments contribute to your **Primary Goal**? If
so, how? _____
_____

WEEKLY GOAL SETTING:

Refer to the previous page when completing this section.
If you did not meet your **Mini Goal**, what obstacles prevented you from doing so? _____

_____

_____

What **Action Steps** helped the most with your goal? Why?____

_____

_____

Do you need to repeat any **Action Steps** to help develop a habit? Which ones? _____

_____

What did you notice and learn?_____

_____

_____

My **Primary Goal** is: _____

The **Mini Goal** that I will work on this week is: _____

_____

Why is this **Mini Goal** important to your goal process?_____

_____

The habit that I would like to focus on to support my goal this week is: _____

Action Steps that I can do to work toward my goal this week are:

_____   _____

_____   _____

_____   _____

*Plan out and list your **Action Steps** and habit goals on the line for each day on the following page. As you complete these tasks, check them off!*

NEW WEEK + NEW FOCUS = NEW YOU:

My **Primary Goal** is: _____

It is important that I reach this goal because: _____

_____

_____

Each day list three things that make you feel grateful.

MONTH / DAY	1 _____
	2 _____
	3 _____

Action Step _____ Complete ❏

Habit goal _____ Complete ❏

Notes _____

MONTH / DAY	1 _____
	2 _____
	3 _____

Action Step _____ Complete ❏

Habit goal _____ Complete ❏

Notes _____

MONTH / DAY	1 _____
	2 _____
	3 _____

Action Step _____ Complete ❏

Habit goal _____ Complete ❏

Notes _____

MONTH / DAY

1 _____
2 _____
3 _____

Action Step _____ Complete ❏
Habit goal _____ Complete ❏
Notes _____

MONTH / DAY

1 _____
2 _____
3 _____

Action Step _____ Complete ❏
Habit goal _____ Complete ❏
Notes _____

MONTH / DAY

1 _____
2 _____
3 _____

Action Step _____ Complete ❏
Habit goal _____ Complete ❏
Notes _____

MONTH / DAY

1 _____
2 _____
3 _____

Action Step _____ Complete ❏
Habit goal _____ Complete ❏
Notes _____

WEEKLY RECAP – GOALS:

Did you meet your **Mini Goal** for this week? ❏ Yes ❏ No

If no, do you need to spend another week on this **Mini Goal** or would you prefer to move onto a new **Mini Goal** and return to this **Mini Goal** another time? ❏ Same ❏ New

If you answered "Yes," which goal would you like to work on this week?_____

What **Action Steps** helped the most toward achieving your goal? _____

_____

Do you need to repeat any **Action Steps** to develop a habit?

_____

What did you notice and learn?_____

WEEKLY RECAP – GRATITUDE:

Without looking back at what you have written down during the past week, answer the following questions:

What was the best part of your week? _____

_____

Who did you enjoy spending time with this week? _____

_____

Now look back at what you have written for the last week. What do you notice about how you feel today versus how you felt in the moment? _____

_____

Did any of these moments contribute to your **Primary Goal**? If so, how? _____

_____

WEEKLY GOAL SETTING:

Refer to the previous page when completing this section.

If you did not meet your **Mini Goal**, what obstacles prevented you from doing so? _____

_____

_____

What **Action Steps** helped the most with your goal? Why?____

_____

_____

Do you need to repeat any **Action Steps** to help develop a habit? Which ones? _____

_____

What did you notice and learn?_____

_____

_____

My **Primary Goal** is: _____

The **Mini Goal** that I will work on this week is: _____

_____

Why is this **Mini Goal** important to your goal process?_____

_____

The habit that I would like to focus on to support my goal this week is: _____

Action Steps that I can do to work toward my goal this week are:

_____   _____

_____   _____

_____   _____

*Plan out and list your **Action Steps** and habit goals on the line for each day on the following page. As you complete these tasks, check them off!*

NEW WEEK + NEW FOCUS = NEW YOU:

My **Primary Goal** is: _____

It is important that I reach this goal because: _____

_____

_____

Each day list three things that make you feel grateful.

```
┌─────────┐
│ MONTH ╱ │   1 _____
│      ╱  │
│     ╱   │   2 _____
│    ╱ DAY│
└─────────┘   3 _____
```

Action Step _____ Complete ❏

Habit goal _____ Complete ❏

Notes _____

```
┌─────────┐
│ MONTH ╱ │   1 _____
│      ╱  │
│     ╱   │   2 _____
│    ╱ DAY│
└─────────┘   3 _____
```

Action Step _____ Complete ❏

Habit goal _____ Complete ❏

Notes _____

```
┌─────────┐
│ MONTH ╱ │   1 _____
│      ╱  │
│     ╱   │   2 _____
│    ╱ DAY│
└─────────┘   3 _____
```

Action Step _____ Complete ❏

Habit goal _____ Complete ❏

Notes _____

MONTH ⟋	1 _____
⟋	2 _____
⟋ DAY	3 _____

Action Step _____ Complete ❑

Habit goal _____ Complete ❑

Notes _____

MONTH ⟋	1 _____
⟋	2 _____
⟋ DAY	3 _____

Action Step _____ Complete ❑

Habit goal _____ Complete ❑

Notes _____

MONTH ⟋	1 _____
⟋	2 _____
⟋ DAY	3 _____

Action Step _____ Complete ❑

Habit goal _____ Complete ❑

Notes _____

MONTH ⟋	1 _____
⟋	2 _____
⟋ DAY	3 _____

Action Step _____ Complete ❑

Habit goal _____ Complete ❑

Notes _____

WEEKLY RECAP – GOALS:

Did you meet your **Mini Goal** for this week? ❑ Yes ❑ No
If no, do you need to spend another week on this **Mini Goal**
or would you prefer to move onto a new **Mini Goal** and return
to this **Mini Goal** another time? ❑ Same ❑ New
If you answered "Yes," which goal would you like to work on
this week?_____
What **Action Steps** helped the most toward achieving your
goal? _____
_____
Do you need to repeat any **Action Steps** to develop a habit?
_____
What did you notice and learn?_____
_____

WEEKLY RECAP – GRATITUDE:

Without looking back at what you have written down during
the past week, answer the following questions:
What was the best part of your week?_____
_____
Who did you enjoy spending time with this week? _____
_____
Now look back at what you have written for the last week.
What do you notice about how you feel today versus how you
felt in the moment? _____
_____
Did any of these moments contribute to your **Primary Goal**? If
so, how? _____
_____

WEEKLY GOAL SETTING:

Refer to the previous page when completing this section.
If you did not meet your **Mini Goal**, what obstacles prevented
you from doing so? _____

_____

_____

What **Action Steps** helped the most with your goal? Why?____

_____

_____

Do you need to repeat any **Action Steps** to help develop a
habit? Which ones? _____

_____

What did you notice and learn?_____

_____

_____

My **Primary Goal** is: _____

The **Mini Goal** that I will work on this week is: _____

_____

Why is this **Mini Goal** important to your goal process?_____

_____

The habit that I would like to focus on to support my goal this
week is: _____

Action Steps that I can do to work toward my goal this week are:

_____   _____

_____   _____

_____   _____

Plan out and list your **Action Steps** *and habit goals on the line for each
day on the following page. As you complete these tasks, check them off!*

NEW WEEK + NEW FOCUS = NEW YOU:

My **Primary Goal** is: _____

It is important that I reach this goal because: _____

_____

_____

Each day list three things that make you feel grateful.

MONTH / DAY	1 _____
	2 _____
	3 _____

Action Step _____ Complete ❑

Habit goal _____ Complete ❑

Notes _____

MONTH / DAY	1 _____
	2 _____
	3 _____

Action Step _____ Complete ❑

Habit goal _____ Complete ❑

Notes _____

MONTH / DAY	1 _____
	2 _____
	3 _____

Action Step _____ Complete ❑

Habit goal _____ Complete ❑

Notes _____

MONTH / DAY

1 _____
2 _____
3 _____

Action Step _____ Complete ❏

Habit goal _____ Complete ❏

Notes _____

MONTH / DAY

1 _____
2 _____
3 _____

Action Step _____ Complete ❏

Habit goal _____ Complete ❏

Notes _____

MONTH / DAY

1 _____
2 _____
3 _____

Action Step _____ Complete ❏

Habit goal _____ Complete ❏

Notes _____

MONTH / DAY

1 _____
2 _____
3 _____

Action Step _____ Complete ❏

Habit goal _____ Complete ❏

Notes _____

WEEKLY RECAP – GOALS:

Did you meet your **Mini Goal** for this week? ❏ Yes ❏ No
If no, do you need to spend another week on this **Mini Goal**
or would you prefer to move onto a new **Mini Goal** and return
to this **Mini Goal** another time? ❏ Same ❏ New
If you answered "Yes," which goal would you like to work on
this week?_____
What **Action Steps** helped the most toward achieving your
goal? _____

_____

Do you need to repeat any **Action Steps** to develop a habit?

_____

What did you notice and learn?_____

_____

WEEKLY RECAP – GRATITUDE:

Without looking back at what you have written down during
the past week, answer the following questions:
What was the best part of your week?_____

_____

Who did you enjoy spending time with this week? _____

_____

Now look back at what you have written for the last week.
What do you notice about how you feel today versus how you
felt in the moment? _____

_____

Did any of these moments contribute to your **Primary Goal**? If
so, how? _____

_____

WEEKLY GOAL SETTING:

Refer to the previous page when completing this section.

If you did not meet your **Mini Goal**, what obstacles prevented you from doing so? _____

_____

_____

What **Action Steps** helped the most with your goal? Why?____

_____

_____

Do you need to repeat any **Action Steps** to help develop a habit? Which ones? _____

_____

What did you notice and learn?_____

_____

_____

My **Primary Goal** is: _____

The **Mini Goal** that I will work on this week is: _____

_____

Why is this **Mini Goal** important to your goal process?_____

_____

The habit that I would like to focus on to support my goal this week is: _____

Action Steps that I can do to work toward my goal this week are:

_____   _____

_____   _____

_____   _____

Plan out and list your **Action Steps** *and habit goals on the line for each day on the following page. As you complete these tasks, check them off!*

NEW WEEK + NEW FOCUS = NEW YOU:

My **Primary Goal** is: _____

It is important that I reach this goal because: _____

_____

_____

Each day list three things that make you feel grateful.

MONTH / DAY	1 _____
	2 _____
	3 _____

Action Step _____ Complete ❏

Habit goal _____ Complete ❏

Notes _____

MONTH / DAY	1 _____
	2 _____
	3 _____

Action Step _____ Complete ❏

Habit goal _____ Complete ❏

Notes _____

MONTH / DAY	1 _____
	2 _____
	3 _____

Action Step _____ Complete ❏

Habit goal _____ Complete ❏

Notes _____

MONTH / DAY	1 _____
	2 _____
	3 _____

Action Step _____ Complete ❑

Habit goal _____ Complete ❑

Notes _____

MONTH / DAY	1 _____
	2 _____
	3 _____

Action Step _____ Complete ❑

Habit goal _____ Complete ❑

Notes _____

MONTH / DAY	1 _____
	2 _____
	3 _____

Action Step _____ Complete ❑

Habit goal _____ Complete ❑

Notes _____

MONTH / DAY	1 _____
	2 _____
	3 _____

Action Step _____ Complete ❑

Habit goal _____ Complete ❑

Notes _____

WEEKLY RECAP – GOALS:

Did you meet your **Mini Goal** for this week? ❏ Yes ❏ No

If no, do you need to spend another week on this **Mini Goal** or would you prefer to move onto a new **Mini Goal** and return to this **Mini Goal** another time? ❏ Same ❏ New

If you answered "Yes," which goal would you like to work on this week?_____

What **Action Steps** helped the most toward achieving your goal? _____

_____

Do you need to repeat any **Action Steps** to develop a habit?

_____

What did you notice and learn?_____

_____

WEEKLY RECAP – GRATITUDE:

Without looking back at what you have written down during the past week, answer the following questions:

What was the best part of your week?_____

_____

Who did you enjoy spending time with this week? _____

_____

Now look back at what you have written for the last week. What do you notice about how you feel today versus how you felt in the moment? _____

_____

Did any of these moments contribute to your **Primary Goal**? If so, how? _____

_____

WEEKLY GOAL SETTING:

Refer to the previous page when completing this section.

If you did not meet your **Mini Goal**, what obstacles prevented you from doing so? _____

_____

_____

What **Action Steps** helped the most with your goal? Why?____

_____

_____

Do you need to repeat any **Action Steps** to help develop a habit? Which ones? _____

_____

What did you notice and learn?_____

_____

_____

My **Primary Goal** is: _____

The **Mini Goal** that I will work on this week is: _____

_____

Why is this **Mini Goal** important to your goal process?_____

_____

The habit that I would like to focus on to support my goal this week is: _____

Action Steps that I can do to work toward my goal this week are:

_____   _____

_____   _____

_____   _____

Plan out and list your **Action Steps** *and habit goals on the line for each day on the following page. As you complete these tasks, check them off!*

NEW WEEK + NEW FOCUS = NEW YOU:

My **Primary Goal** is: _____

It is important that I reach this goal because: _____

_____

_____

Each day list three things that make you feel grateful.

MONTH / DAY	1 _____
	2 _____
	3 _____

Action Step _____ Complete ❑

Habit goal _____ Complete ❑

Notes _____

MONTH / DAY	1 _____
	2 _____
	3 _____

Action Step _____ Complete ❑

Habit goal _____ Complete ❑

Notes _____

MONTH / DAY	1 _____
	2 _____
	3 _____

Action Step _____ Complete ❑

Habit goal _____ Complete ❑

Notes _____

MONTH / DAY

1 _____
2 _____
3 _____

Action Step _____ Complete ❑
Habit goal _____ Complete ❑
Notes _____

MONTH / DAY

1 _____
2 _____
3 _____

Action Step _____ Complete ❑
Habit goal _____ Complete ❑
Notes _____

MONTH / DAY

1 _____
2 _____
3 _____

Action Step _____ Complete ❑
Habit goal _____ Complete ❑
Notes _____

MONTH / DAY

1 _____
2 _____
3 _____

Action Step _____ Complete ❑
Habit goal _____ Complete ❑
Notes _____

WEEKLY RECAP – GOALS:

Did you meet your **Mini Goal** for this week? ❑ Yes ❑ No
If no, do you need to spend another week on this **Mini Goal**
or would you prefer to move onto a new **Mini Goal** and return
to this **Mini Goal** another time? ❑ Same ❑ New
If you answered "Yes," which goal would you like to work on
this week?_____
What **Action Steps** helped the most toward achieving your
goal? _____
_____
Do you need to repeat any **Action Steps** to develop a habit?
_____
What did you notice and learn?_____
_____

WEEKLY RECAP – GRATITUDE:

Without looking back at what you have written down during
the past week, answer the following questions:
What was the best part of your week?_____
_____
Who did you enjoy spending time with this week? _____
_____
Now look back at what you have written for the last week.
What do you notice about how you feel today versus how you
felt in the moment? _____
_____
Did any of these moments contribute to your **Primary Goal**? If
so, how? _____
_____

WEEKLY GOAL SETTING:

Refer to the previous page when completing this section.

If you did not meet your **Mini Goal**, what obstacles prevented you from doing so? _____

_____

_____

What **Action Steps** helped the most with your goal? Why?____

_____

_____

Do you need to repeat any **Action Steps** to help develop a habit? Which ones? _____

_____

What did you notice and learn?_____

_____

_____

My **Primary Goal** is: _____

The **Mini Goal** that I will work on this week is: _____

_____

Why is this **Mini Goal** important to your goal process?_____

_____

The habit that I would like to focus on to support my goal this week is: _____

Action Steps that I can do to work toward my goal this week are:

_____   _____

_____   _____

_____   _____

*Plan out and list your **Action Steps** and habit goals on the line for each day on the following page. As you complete these tasks, check them off!*

NEW WEEK + NEW FOCUS = NEW YOU:

My **Primary Goal** is: _____

It is important that I reach this goal because: _____

_____

_____

Each day list three things that make you feel grateful.

MONTH / DAY	1 _____
	2 _____
	3 _____

Action Step _____ Complete ❏

Habit goal _____ Complete ❏

Notes _____

MONTH / DAY	1 _____
	2 _____
	3 _____

Action Step _____ Complete ❏

Habit goal _____ Complete ❏

Notes _____

MONTH / DAY	1 _____
	2 _____
	3 _____

Action Step _____ Complete ❏

Habit goal _____ Complete ❏

Notes _____

```
┌──────────┐
│ MONTH  ╱ │   1 _____
│      ╱   │   2 _____
│    ╱  DAY│   3 _____
└──────────┘
```

Action Step _____ Complete ❏

Habit goal _____ Complete ❏

Notes _____

```
┌──────────┐
│ MONTH  ╱ │   1 _____
│      ╱   │   2 _____
│    ╱  DAY│   3 _____
└──────────┘
```

Action Step _____ Complete ❏

Habit goal _____ Complete ❏

Notes _____

```
┌──────────┐
│ MONTH  ╱ │   1 _____
│      ╱   │   2 _____
│    ╱  DAY│   3 _____
└──────────┘
```

Action Step _____ Complete ❏

Habit goal _____ Complete ❏

Notes _____

```
┌──────────┐
│ MONTH  ╱ │   1 _____
│      ╱   │   2 _____
│    ╱  DAY│   3 _____
└──────────┘
```

Action Step _____ Complete ❏

Habit goal _____ Complete ❏

Notes _____

WEEKLY RECAP – GOALS:

Did you meet your **Mini Goal** for this week? ❑ Yes ❑ No
If no, do you need to spend another week on this **Mini Goal**
or would you prefer to move onto a new **Mini Goal** and return
to this **Mini Goal** another time? ❑ Same ❑ New
If you answered "Yes," which goal would you like to work on
this week?_____
What **Action Steps** helped the most toward achieving your
goal? _____

_____

Do you need to repeat any **Action Steps** to develop a habit?

_____

What did you notice and learn?_____

WEEKLY RECAP – GRATITUDE:

Without looking back at what you have written down during
the past week, answer the following questions:
What was the best part of your week?_____

_____

Who did you enjoy spending time with this week? _____

_____

Now look back at what you have written for the last week.
What do you notice about how you feel today versus how you
felt in the moment? _____

_____

Did any of these moments contribute to your **Primary Goal**? If
so, how? _____

_____

WEEKLY GOAL SETTING:

Refer to the previous page when completing this section.
If you did not meet your **Mini Goal**, what obstacles prevented you from doing so? _____

_____

_____

What **Action Steps** helped the most with your goal? Why?____

_____

_____

Do you need to repeat any **Action Steps** to help develop a habit? Which ones? _____

_____

What did you notice and learn?_____

_____

_____

My **Primary Goal** is: _____
The **Mini Goal** that I will work on this week is: _____

_____

Why is this **Mini Goal** important to your goal process?_____

_____

The habit that I would like to focus on to support my goal this week is: _____

Action Steps that I can do to work toward my goal this week are:

_____   _____

_____   _____

_____   _____

Plan out and list your **Action Steps** *and habit goals on the line for each day on the following page. As you complete these tasks, check them off!*

NEW WEEK + NEW FOCUS = NEW YOU:

My **Primary Goal** is: _____

It is important that I reach this goal because: _____

_____

_____

Each day list three things that make you feel grateful.

MONTH / DAY	1 _____
	2 _____
	3 _____

Action Step _____ Complete ❏

Habit goal   _____ Complete ❏

Notes _____

MONTH / DAY	1 _____
	2 _____
	3 _____

Action Step _____ Complete ❏

Habit goal   _____ Complete ❏

Notes _____

MONTH / DAY	1 _____
	2 _____
	3 _____

Action Step _____ Complete ❏

Habit goal   _____ Complete ❏

Notes _____

MONTH / DAY	1 _____
	2 _____
	3 _____

Action Step _____ Complete ❑

Habit goal _____ Complete ❑

Notes _____

MONTH / DAY	1 _____
	2 _____
	3 _____

Action Step _____ Complete ❑

Habit goal _____ Complete ❑

Notes _____

MONTH / DAY	1 _____
	2 _____
	3 _____

Action Step _____ Complete ❑

Habit goal _____ Complete ❑

Notes _____

MONTH / DAY	1 _____
	2 _____
	3 _____

Action Step _____ Complete ❑

Habit goal _____ Complete ❑

Notes _____

WEEKLY RECAP – GOALS:

Did you meet your **Mini Goal** for this week? ❑ Yes ❑ No

If no, do you need to spend another week on this **Mini Goal** or would you prefer to move onto a new **Mini Goal** and return to this **Mini Goal** another time? ❑ Same ❑ New

If you answered "Yes," which goal would you like to work on this week?_____

What **Action Steps** helped the most toward achieving your goal? _____

_____

Do you need to repeat any **Action Steps** to develop a habit?

_____

What did you notice and learn?_____

_____

WEEKLY RECAP – GRATITUDE:

Without looking back at what you have written down during the past week, answer the following questions:

What was the best part of your week?_____

_____

Who did you enjoy spending time with this week? _____

_____

Now look back at what you have written for the last week. What do you notice about how you feel today versus how you felt in the moment? _____

_____

Did any of these moments contribute to your **Primary Goal**? If so, how? _____

_____

WEEKLY GOAL SETTING:

Refer to the previous page when completing this section.

If you did not meet your **Mini Goal**, what obstacles prevented you from doing so? _____

_____

_____

What **Action Steps** helped the most with your goal? Why?____

_____

_____

Do you need to repeat any **Action Steps** to help develop a habit? Which ones? _____

_____

What did you notice and learn?_____

_____

_____

My **Primary Goal** is: _____

The **Mini Goal** that I will work on this week is: _____

_____

Why is this **Mini Goal** important to your goal process?_____

_____

The habit that I would like to focus on to support my goal this week is: _____

Action Steps that I can do to work toward my goal this week are:

_____   _____

_____   _____

_____   _____

Plan out and list your **Action Steps** *and habit goals on the line for each day on the following page. As you complete these tasks, check them off!*

NEW WEEK + NEW FOCUS = NEW YOU:

My **Primary Goal** is: _____

It is important that I reach this goal because: _____

_____

_____

Each day list three things that make you feel grateful.

MONTH / DAY	
	1 _____
	2 _____
	3 _____

Action Step _____ Complete ❑

Habit goal _____ Complete ❑

Notes _____

MONTH / DAY	
	1 _____
	2 _____
	3 _____

Action Step _____ Complete ❑

Habit goal _____ Complete ❑

Notes _____

MONTH / DAY	
	1 _____
	2 _____
	3 _____

Action Step _____ Complete ❑

Habit goal _____ Complete ❑

Notes _____

MONTH / DAY	1 _____
	2 _____
	3 _____

Action Step _____ Complete ❏

Habit goal _____ Complete ❏

Notes _____

MONTH / DAY	1 _____
	2 _____
	3 _____

Action Step _____ Complete ❏

Habit goal _____ Complete ❏

Notes _____

MONTH / DAY	1 _____
	2 _____
	3 _____

Action Step _____ Complete ❏

Habit goal _____ Complete ❏

Notes _____

MONTH / DAY	1 _____
	2 _____
	3 _____

Action Step _____ Complete ❏

Habit goal _____ Complete ❏

Notes _____

WEEKLY RECAP – GOALS:

Did you meet your **Mini Goal** for this week? ❑ Yes ❑ No
If no, do you need to spend another week on this **Mini Goal**
or would you prefer to move onto a new **Mini Goal** and return
to this **Mini Goal** another time? ❑ Same ❑ New
If you answered "Yes," which goal would you like to work on
this week?_____
What **Action Steps** helped the most toward achieving your
goal? _____
_____
Do you need to repeat any **Action Steps** to develop a habit?
_____
What did you notice and learn?_____

WEEKLY RECAP – GRATITUDE:

Without looking back at what you have written down during
the past week, answer the following questions:
What was the best part of your week?_____
_____
Who did you enjoy spending time with this week? _____
_____
Now look back at what you have written for the last week.
What do you notice about how you feel today versus how you
felt in the moment? _____
_____
Did any of these moments contribute to your **Primary Goal**? If
so, how? _____
_____

WEEKLY GOAL SETTING:

Refer to the previous page when completing this section.
If you did not meet your **Mini Goal**, what obstacles prevented you from doing so? _____

_____

_____

What **Action Steps** helped the most with your goal? Why?____

_____

_____

Do you need to repeat any **Action Steps** to help develop a habit? Which ones? _____

_____

What did you notice and learn?_____

_____

_____

My **Primary Goal** is: _____

The **Mini Goal** that I will work on this week is: _____

_____

Why is this **Mini Goal** important to your goal process?_____

_____

The habit that I would like to focus on to support my goal this week is: _____

Action Steps that I can do to work toward my goal this week are:

_____   _____

_____   _____

_____   _____

Plan out and list your **Action Steps** *and habit goals on the line for each day on the following page. As you complete these tasks, check them off!*

NEW WEEK + NEW FOCUS = NEW YOU:

My **Primary Goal** is: _____

It is important that I reach this goal because: _____

_____

_____

Each day list three things that make you feel grateful.

MONTH / DAY	1 _____
	2 _____
	3 _____

Action Step _____ Complete ❑

Habit goal _____ Complete ❑

Notes _____

MONTH / DAY	1 _____
	2 _____
	3 _____

Action Step _____ Complete ❑

Habit goal _____ Complete ❑

Notes _____

MONTH / DAY	1 _____
	2 _____
	3 _____

Action Step _____ Complete ❑

Habit goal _____ Complete ❑

Notes _____

MONTH	1 _____
	2 _____
DAY	3 _____

Action Step _____ Complete ❑

Habit goal _____ Complete ❑

Notes _____

MONTH	1 _____
	2 _____
DAY	3 _____

Action Step _____ Complete ❑

Habit goal _____ Complete ❑

Notes _____

MONTH	1 _____
	2 _____
DAY	3 _____

Action Step _____ Complete ❑

Habit goal _____ Complete ❑

Notes _____

MONTH	1 _____
	2 _____
DAY	3 _____

Action Step _____ Complete ❑

Habit goal _____ Complete ❑

Notes _____

WEEKLY RECAP – GOALS:

Did you meet your **Mini Goal** for this week? ❑ Yes ❑ No

If no, do you need to spend another week on this **Mini Goal** or would you prefer to move onto a new **Mini Goal** and return to this **Mini Goal** another time? ❑ Same ❑ New

If you answered "Yes," which goal would you like to work on this week?_____

What **Action Steps** helped the most toward achieving your goal? _____

_____

Do you need to repeat any **Action Steps** to develop a habit?

_____

What did you notice and learn?_____

_____

WEEKLY RECAP – GRATITUDE:

Without looking back at what you have written down during the past week, answer the following questions:

What was the best part of your week?_____

_____

Who did you enjoy spending time with this week? _____

_____

Now look back at what you have written for the last week.

What do you notice about how you feel today versus how you felt in the moment? _____

_____

Did any of these moments contribute to your **Primary Goal**? If so, how? _____

_____

WEEKLY GOAL SETTING:

Refer to the previous page when completing this section.

If you did not meet your **Mini Goal**, what obstacles prevented you from doing so? _____

_____

_____

What **Action Steps** helped the most with your goal? Why?____

_____

_____

Do you need to repeat any **Action Steps** to help develop a habit? Which ones? _____

_____

What did you notice and learn?_____

_____

_____

My **Primary Goal** is: _____

The **Mini Goal** that I will work on this week is: _____

_____

Why is this **Mini Goal** important to your goal process?_____

_____

The habit that I would like to focus on to support my goal this week is: _____

Action Steps that I can do to work toward my goal this week are:

_____   _____

_____   _____

_____   _____

*Plan out and list your **Action Steps** and habit goals on the line for each day on the following page. As you complete these tasks, check them off!*

NEW WEEK + NEW FOCUS = NEW YOU:

My **Primary Goal** is: _____

It is important that I reach this goal because: _____

_____

_____

Each day list three things that make you feel grateful.

MONTH / DAY	1 _____
	2 _____
	3 _____

Action Step _____ Complete ❏

Habit goal _____ Complete ❏

Notes _____

MONTH / DAY	1 _____
	2 _____
	3 _____

Action Step _____ Complete ❏

Habit goal _____ Complete ❏

Notes _____

MONTH / DAY	1 _____
	2 _____
	3 _____

Action Step _____ Complete ❏

Habit goal _____ Complete ❏

Notes _____

MONTH / DAY	1 _____
	2 _____
	3 _____

Action Step _____ Complete ❑

Habit goal _____ Complete ❑

Notes _____

MONTH / DAY	1 _____
	2 _____
	3 _____

Action Step _____ Complete ❑

Habit goal _____ Complete ❑

Notes _____

MONTH / DAY	1 _____
	2 _____
	3 _____

Action Step _____ Complete ❑

Habit goal _____ Complete ❑

Notes _____

MONTH / DAY	1 _____
	2 _____
	3 _____

Action Step _____ Complete ❑

Habit goal _____ Complete ❑

Notes _____

WEEKLY RECAP – GOALS:

Did you meet your **Mini Goal** for this week? ❏ Yes ❏ No
If no, do you need to spend another week on this **Mini Goal**
or would you prefer to move onto a new **Mini Goal** and return
to this **Mini Goal** another time? ❏ Same ❏ New
If you answered "Yes," which goal would you like to work on
this week?_____
What **Action Steps** helped the most toward achieving your
goal? _____
_____
Do you need to repeat any **Action Steps** to develop a habit?
_____
What did you notice and learn?_____
_____

WEEKLY RECAP – GRATITUDE:

Without looking back at what you have written down during
the past week, answer the following questions:
What was the best part of your week?_____
_____
Who did you enjoy spending time with this week? _____
_____
Now look back at what you have written for the last week.
What do you notice about how you feel today versus how you
felt in the moment? _____
_____
Did any of these moments contribute to your **Primary Goal**? If
so, how? _____
_____

WEEKLY GOAL SETTING:

Refer to the previous page when completing this section.

If you did not meet your **Mini Goal**, what obstacles prevented you from doing so? _____

_____

_____

What **Action Steps** helped the most with your goal? Why?____

_____

_____

Do you need to repeat any **Action Steps** to help develop a habit? Which ones? _____

_____

What did you notice and learn?_____

_____

_____

My **Primary Goal** is: _____

The **Mini Goal** that I will work on this week is: _____

_____

Why is this **Mini Goal** important to your goal process?_____

_____

The habit that I would like to focus on to support my goal this week is: _____

Action Steps that I can do to work toward my goal this week are:

_____   _____

_____   _____

_____   _____

*Plan out and list your **Action Steps** and habit goals on the line for each day on the following page. As you complete these tasks, check them off!*

NEW WEEK + NEW FOCUS = NEW YOU:

My **Primary Goal** is: _____

It is important that I reach this goal because: _____

_____

_____

Each day list three things that make you feel grateful.

MONTH / DAY

1 _____

2 _____

3 _____

Action Step _____ Complete ❑

Habit goal _____ Complete ❑

Notes _____

MONTH / DAY

1 _____

2 _____

3 _____

Action Step _____ Complete ❑

Habit goal _____ Complete ❑

Notes _____

MONTH / DAY

1 _____

2 _____

3 _____

Action Step _____ Complete ❑

Habit goal _____ Complete ❑

Notes _____

MONTH / DAY	1 _____
	2 _____
	3 _____

Action Step _____ Complete ❏

Habit goal _____ Complete ❏

Notes _____

MONTH / DAY	1 _____
	2 _____
	3 _____

Action Step _____ Complete ❏

Habit goal _____ Complete ❏

Notes _____

MONTH / DAY	1 _____
	2 _____
	3 _____

Action Step _____ Complete ❏

Habit goal _____ Complete ❏

Notes _____

MONTH / DAY	1 _____
	2 _____
	3 _____

Action Step _____ Complete ❏

Habit goal _____ Complete ❏

Notes _____

WEEKLY RECAP – GOALS:

Did you meet your **Mini Goal** for this week? ❏ Yes ❏ No

If no, do you need to spend another week on this **Mini Goal**
or would you prefer to move onto a new **Mini Goal** and return
to this **Mini Goal** another time? ❏ Same ❏ New

If you answered "Yes," which goal would you like to work on
this week?_____

What **Action Steps** helped the most toward achieving your
goal? _____

_____

Do you need to repeat any **Action Steps** to develop a habit?

_____

What did you notice and learn?_____

_____

WEEKLY RECAP – GRATITUDE:

Without looking back at what you have written down during
the past week, answer the following questions:

What was the best part of your week?_____

_____

Who did you enjoy spending time with this week? _____

_____

Now look back at what you have written for the last week.
What do you notice about how you feel today versus how you
felt in the moment? _____

_____

Did any of these moments contribute to your **Primary Goal**? If
so, how? _____

_____

WEEKLY GOAL SETTING:

Refer to the previous page when completing this section.

If you did not meet your **Mini Goal**, what obstacles prevented you from doing so? _____

_____

_____

What **Action Steps** helped the most with your goal? Why?____

_____

_____

Do you need to repeat any **Action Steps** to help develop a habit? Which ones? _____

_____

What did you notice and learn?_____

_____

_____

My **Primary Goal** is: _____

The **Mini Goal** that I will work on this week is: _____

_____

Why is this **Mini Goal** important to your goal process?_____

_____

The habit that I would like to focus on to support my goal this week is: _____

Action Steps that I can do to work toward my goal this week are:

_____   _____

_____   _____

_____   _____

Plan out and list your **Action Steps** *and habit goals on the line for each day on the following page. As you complete these tasks, check them off!*

NEW WEEK + NEW FOCUS = NEW YOU:

My **Primary Goal** is: _____

It is important that I reach this goal because: _____

_____

_____

Each day list three things that make you feel grateful.

| MONTH / DAY | 1 _____ |
| 2 _____ |
| 3 _____ |

Action Step _____ Complete ❏

Habit goal _____ Complete ❏

Notes _____

| MONTH / DAY | 1 _____ |
| 2 _____ |
| 3 _____ |

Action Step _____ Complete ❏

Habit goal _____ Complete ❏

Notes _____

| MONTH / DAY | 1 _____ |
| 2 _____ |
| 3 _____ |

Action Step _____ Complete ❏

Habit goal _____ Complete ❏

Notes _____

MONTH / DAY	1 _____
	2 _____
	3 _____

Action Step _____ Complete ❑

Habit goal _____ Complete ❑

Notes _____

MONTH / DAY	1 _____
	2 _____
	3 _____

Action Step _____ Complete ❑

Habit goal _____ Complete ❑

Notes _____

MONTH / DAY	1 _____
	2 _____
	3 _____

Action Step _____ Complete ❑

Habit goal _____ Complete ❑

Notes _____

MONTH / DAY	1 _____
	2 _____
	3 _____

Action Step _____ Complete ❑

Habit goal _____ Complete ❑

Notes _____

WEEKLY RECAP – GOALS:

Did you meet your **Mini Goal** for this week? ❏ Yes ❏ No

If no, do you need to spend another week on this **Mini Goal** or would you prefer to move onto a new **Mini Goal** and return to this **Mini Goal** another time? ❏ Same ❏ New

If you answered "Yes," which goal would you like to work on this week?_____

What **Action Steps** helped the most toward achieving your goal? _____

_____

Do you need to repeat any **Action Steps** to develop a habit?

_____

What did you notice and learn?_____

_____

WEEKLY RECAP – GRATITUDE:

Without looking back at what you have written down during the past week, answer the following questions:

What was the best part of your week?_____

_____

Who did you enjoy spending time with this week? _____

_____

Now look back at what you have written for the last week. What do you notice about how you feel today versus how you felt in the moment? _____

_____

Did any of these moments contribute to your **Primary Goal**? If so, how? _____

_____

WEEKLY GOAL SETTING:

Refer to the previous page when completing this section.

If you did not meet your **Mini Goal**, what obstacles prevented you from doing so? _____

_____

_____

What **Action Steps** helped the most with your goal? Why?____

_____

_____

Do you need to repeat any **Action Steps** to help develop a habit? Which ones? _____

_____

What did you notice and learn?_____

_____

_____

My **Primary Goal** is: _____

The **Mini Goal** that I will work on this week is: _____

_____

Why is this **Mini Goal** important to your goal process?_____

_____

The habit that I would like to focus on to support my goal this week is: _____

Action Steps that I can do to work toward my goal this week are:

_____   _____

_____   _____

_____   _____

Plan out and list your **Action Steps** *and habit goals on the line for each day on the following page. As you complete these tasks, check them off!*

NEW WEEK + NEW FOCUS = NEW YOU:

My **Primary Goal** is: _____

It is important that I reach this goal because: _____

_____

_____

Each day list three things that make you feel grateful.

MONTH / DAY	1 _____
	2 _____
	3 _____

Action Step _____ Complete ❏

Habit goal _____ Complete ❏

Notes _____

MONTH / DAY	1 _____
	2 _____
	3 _____

Action Step _____ Complete ❏

Habit goal _____ Complete ❏

Notes _____

MONTH / DAY	1 _____
	2 _____
	3 _____

Action Step _____ Complete ❏

Habit goal _____ Complete ❏

Notes _____

MONTH / DAY	1 _____
	2 _____
	3 _____

Action Step _____ Complete ❑

Habit goal _____ Complete ❑

Notes _____

MONTH / DAY	1 _____
	2 _____
	3 _____

Action Step _____ Complete ❑

Habit goal _____ Complete ❑

Notes _____

MONTH / DAY	1 _____
	2 _____
	3 _____

Action Step _____ Complete ❑

Habit goal _____ Complete ❑

Notes _____

MONTH / DAY	1 _____
	2 _____
	3 _____

Action Step _____ Complete ❑

Habit goal _____ Complete ❑

Notes _____

WEEKLY RECAP – GOALS:

Did you meet your **Mini Goal** for this week? ❏ Yes ❏ No

If no, do you need to spend another week on this **Mini Goal** or would you prefer to move onto a new **Mini Goal** and return to this **Mini Goal** another time? ❏ Same ❏ New

If you answered "Yes," which goal would you like to work on this week?_____

What **Action Steps** helped the most toward achieving your goal? _____

_____

Do you need to repeat any **Action Steps** to develop a habit?

_____

What did you notice and learn?_____

WEEKLY RECAP – GRATITUDE:

Without looking back at what you have written down during the past week, answer the following questions:

What was the best part of your week? _____

_____

Who did you enjoy spending time with this week? _____

_____

Now look back at what you have written for the last week.

What do you notice about how you feel today versus how you felt in the moment? _____

_____

Did any of these moments contribute to your **Primary Goal**? If so, how? _____

_____

WEEKLY GOAL SETTING:

Refer to the previous page when completing this section.

If you did not meet your **Mini Goal**, what obstacles prevented you from doing so? _____

_____

_____

What **Action Steps** helped the most with your goal? Why?____

_____

_____

Do you need to repeat any **Action Steps** to help develop a habit? Which ones? _____

_____

What did you notice and learn?_____

_____

_____

My **Primary Goal** is: _____

The **Mini Goal** that I will work on this week is: _____

_____

Why is this **Mini Goal** important to your goal process?_____

_____

The habit that I would like to focus on to support my goal this week is: _____

Action Steps that I can do to work toward my goal this week are:

_____   _____

_____   _____

_____   _____

*Plan out and list your **Action Steps** and habit goals on the line for each day on the following page. As you complete these tasks, check them off!*

NEW WEEK + NEW FOCUS = NEW YOU:

My **Primary Goal** is: _____

It is important that I reach this goal because: _____

_____

_____

Each day list three things that make you feel grateful.

MONTH / DAY	1 _____
	2 _____
	3 _____

Action Step _____ Complete ❏

Habit goal   _____ Complete ❏

Notes _____

MONTH / DAY	1 _____
	2 _____
	3 _____

Action Step _____ Complete ❏

Habit goal   _____ Complete ❏

Notes _____

MONTH / DAY	1 _____
	2 _____
	3 _____

Action Step _____ Complete ❏

Habit goal   _____ Complete ❏

Notes _____

MONTH		1 _____
	/	2 _____
	DAY	3 _____

Action Step _____ Complete ❏

Habit goal _____ Complete ❏

Notes _____

MONTH		1 _____
	/	2 _____
	DAY	3 _____

Action Step _____ Complete ❏

Habit goal _____ Complete ❏

Notes _____

MONTH		1 _____
	/	2 _____
	DAY	3 _____

Action Step _____ Complete ❏

Habit goal _____ Complete ❏

Notes _____

MONTH		1 _____
	/	2 _____
	DAY	3 _____

Action Step _____ Complete ❏

Habit goal _____ Complete ❏

Notes _____

WEEKLY RECAP – GOALS:

Did you meet your **Mini Goal** for this week? ❏ Yes ❏ No
If no, do you need to spend another week on this **Mini Goal**
or would you prefer to move onto a new **Mini Goal** and return
to this **Mini Goal** another time? ❏ Same ❏ New
If you answered "Yes," which goal would you like to work on
this week?_____
What **Action Steps** helped the most toward achieving your
goal? _____
_____
Do you need to repeat any **Action Steps** to develop a habit?
_____
What did you notice and learn?_____
_____

WEEKLY RECAP – GRATITUDE:

Without looking back at what you have written down during
the past week, answer the following questions:
What was the best part of your week?_____
_____
Who did you enjoy spending time with this week? _____
_____
Now look back at what you have written for the last week.
What do you notice about how you feel today versus how you
felt in the moment? _____
_____
Did any of these moments contribute to your **Primary Goal**? If
so, how? _____
_____

WEEKLY GOAL SETTING:

Refer to the previous page when completing this section.

If you did not meet your **Mini Goal**, what obstacles prevented you from doing so? _____

_____

_____

What **Action Steps** helped the most with your goal? Why?____

_____

_____

Do you need to repeat any **Action Steps** to help develop a habit? Which ones? _____

_____

What did you notice and learn?_____

_____

_____

My **Primary Goal** is: _____

The **Mini Goal** that I will work on this week is: _____

_____

Why is this **Mini Goal** important to your goal process?_____

_____

The habit that I would like to focus on to support my goal this week is: _____

Action Steps that I can do to work toward my goal this week are:

_____   _____

_____   _____

_____   _____

Plan out and list your **Action Steps** *and habit goals on the line for each day on the following page. As you complete these tasks, check them off!*

NEW WEEK + NEW FOCUS = NEW YOU:

My **Primary Goal** is: _____

It is important that I reach this goal because: _____

_____

_____

Each day list three things that make you feel grateful.

MONTH / DAY		
1	_____	
2	_____	
3	_____	

Action Step _____ Complete ❏

Habit goal _____ Complete ❏

Notes _____

MONTH / DAY		
1	_____	
2	_____	
3	_____	

Action Step _____ Complete ❏

Habit goal _____ Complete ❏

Notes _____

MONTH / DAY		
1	_____	
2	_____	
3	_____	

Action Step _____ Complete ❏

Habit goal _____ Complete ❏

Notes _____

MONTH / DAY	1 _____
	2 _____
	3 _____

Action Step _____ Complete ❏

Habit goal _____ Complete ❏

Notes _____

MONTH / DAY	1 _____
	2 _____
	3 _____

Action Step _____ Complete ❏

Habit goal _____ Complete ❏

Notes _____

MONTH / DAY	1 _____
	2 _____
	3 _____

Action Step _____ Complete ❏

Habit goal _____ Complete ❏

Notes _____

MONTH / DAY	1 _____
	2 _____
	3 _____

Action Step _____ Complete ❏

Habit goal _____ Complete ❏

Notes _____

WEEKLY RECAP – GOALS:

Did you meet your **Mini Goal** for this week? ❑ Yes ❑ No

If no, do you need to spend another week on this **Mini Goal** or would you prefer to move onto a new **Mini Goal** and return to this **Mini Goal** another time? ❑ Same ❑ New

If you answered "Yes," which goal would you like to work on this week?_____

What **Action Steps** helped the most toward achieving your goal? _____

_____

Do you need to repeat any **Action Steps** to develop a habit?

_____

What did you notice and learn?_____

WEEKLY RECAP – GRATITUDE:

Without looking back at what you have written down during the past week, answer the following questions:

What was the best part of your week?_____

_____

Who did you enjoy spending time with this week? _____

_____

Now look back at what you have written for the last week. What do you notice about how you feel today versus how you felt in the moment? _____

_____

Did any of these moments contribute to your **Primary Goal**? If so, how? _____

_____

WEEKLY GOAL SETTING:

Refer to the previous page when completing this section.

If you did not meet your **Mini Goal**, what obstacles prevented you from doing so? _____

_____

_____

What **Action Steps** helped the most with your goal? Why?____

_____

_____

Do you need to repeat any **Action Steps** to help develop a habit? Which ones? _____

_____

What did you notice and learn?_____

_____

_____

My **Primary Goal** is: _____

The **Mini Goal** that I will work on this week is: _____

_____

Why is this **Mini Goal** important to your goal process?_____

_____

The habit that I would like to focus on to support my goal this week is: _____

Action Steps that I can do to work toward my goal this week are:

_____   _____

_____   _____

_____   _____

Plan out and list your **Action Steps** *and habit goals on the line for each day on the following page. As you complete these tasks, check them off!*

NEW WEEK + NEW FOCUS = NEW YOU:

My **Primary Goal** is: _____

It is important that I reach this goal because: _____

_____

_____

Each day list three things that make you feel grateful.

MONTH / DAY	1 _____
	2 _____
	3 _____

Action Step _____ Complete ❏

Habit goal   _____ Complete ❏

Notes   _____

MONTH / DAY	1 _____
	2 _____
	3 _____

Action Step _____ Complete ❏

Habit goal   _____ Complete ❏

Notes   _____

MONTH / DAY	1 _____
	2 _____
	3 _____

Action Step _____ Complete ❏

Habit goal   _____ Complete ❏

Notes   _____

MONTH / DAY	1 _____
	2 _____
	3 _____

Action Step _____ Complete ❑

Habit goal _____ Complete ❑

Notes _____

MONTH / DAY	1 _____
	2 _____
	3 _____

Action Step _____ Complete ❑

Habit goal _____ Complete ❑

Notes _____

MONTH / DAY	1 _____
	2 _____
	3 _____

Action Step _____ Complete ❑

Habit goal _____ Complete ❑

Notes _____

MONTH / DAY	1 _____
	2 _____
	3 _____

Action Step _____ Complete ❑

Habit goal _____ Complete ❑

Notes _____

WEEKLY RECAP – GOALS:

Did you meet your **Mini Goal** for this week? ❑ Yes ❑ No
If no, do you need to spend another week on this **Mini Goal**
or would you prefer to move onto a new **Mini Goal** and return
to this **Mini Goal** another time? ❑ Same ❑ New
If you answered "Yes," which goal would you like to work on
this week?_____
What **Action Steps** helped the most toward achieving your
goal? _____

_____

Do you need to repeat any **Action Steps** to develop a habit?

_____

What did you notice and learn?_____

WEEKLY RECAP – GRATITUDE:

Without looking back at what you have written down during
the past week, answer the following questions:
What was the best part of your week? _____

_____

Who did you enjoy spending time with this week? _____

_____

Now look back at what you have written for the last week.
What do you notice about how you feel today versus how you
felt in the moment? _____

_____

Did any of these moments contribute to your **Primary Goal**? If
so, how? _____

_____

WEEKLY GOAL SETTING:

Refer to the previous page when completing this section.

If you did not meet your **Mini Goal**, what obstacles prevented you from doing so? _____

_____

_____

What **Action Steps** helped the most with your goal? Why?____

_____

_____

Do you need to repeat any **Action Steps** to help develop a habit? Which ones? _____

_____

What did you notice and learn?_____

_____

_____

My **Primary Goal** is: _____

The **Mini Goal** that I will work on this week is: _____

_____

Why is this **Mini Goal** important to your goal process?_____

_____

The habit that I would like to focus on to support my goal this week is: _____

Action Steps that I can do to work toward my goal this week are:

_____   _____

_____   _____

_____   _____

*Plan out and list your **Action Steps** and habit goals on the line for each day on the following page. As you complete these tasks, check them off!*

NEW WEEK + NEW FOCUS = NEW YOU:

My **Primary Goal** is: _____

It is important that I reach this goal because: _____

_____

_____

Each day list three things that make you feel grateful.

MONTH / DAY	1 _____
	2 _____
	3 _____

Action Step _____ Complete ❏

Habit goal _____ Complete ❏

Notes _____

MONTH / DAY	1 _____
	2 _____
	3 _____

Action Step _____ Complete ❏

Habit goal _____ Complete ❏

Notes _____

MONTH / DAY	1 _____
	2 _____
	3 _____

Action Step _____ Complete ❏

Habit goal _____ Complete ❏

Notes _____

MONTH / DAY

1 _____
2 _____
3 _____

Action Step _____ Complete ❑

Habit goal _____ Complete ❑

Notes _____

MONTH / DAY

1 _____
2 _____
3 _____

Action Step _____ Complete ❑

Habit goal _____ Complete ❑

Notes _____

MONTH / DAY

1 _____
2 _____
3 _____

Action Step _____ Complete ❑

Habit goal _____ Complete ❑

Notes _____

MONTH / DAY

1 _____
2 _____
3 _____

Action Step _____ Complete ❑

Habit goal _____ Complete ❑

Notes _____

WEEKLY RECAP – GOALS:

Did you meet your **Mini Goal** for this week? ❑ Yes ❑ No
If no, do you need to spend another week on this **Mini Goal**
or would you prefer to move onto a new **Mini Goal** and return
to this **Mini Goal** another time? ❑ Same ❑ New
If you answered "Yes," which goal would you like to work on
this week?_____
What **Action Steps** helped the most toward achieving your
goal? _____

_____
Do you need to repeat any **Action Steps** to develop a habit?

_____
What did you notice and learn?_____

_____

WEEKLY RECAP – GRATITUDE:

Without looking back at what you have written down during
the past week, answer the following questions:
What was the best part of your week?_____

_____
Who did you enjoy spending time with this week? _____

_____
Now look back at what you have written for the last week.
What do you notice about how you feel today versus how you
felt in the moment? _____

_____
Did any of these moments contribute to your **Primary Goal**? If
so, how? _____

_____

WEEKLY GOAL SETTING:

Refer to the previous page when completing this section.
If you did not meet your **Mini Goal**, what obstacles prevented you from doing so? _____

_____

_____

What **Action Steps** helped the most with your goal? Why?____

_____

_____

Do you need to repeat any **Action Steps** to help develop a habit? Which ones? _____

_____

What did you notice and learn?_____

_____

_____

My **Primary Goal** is: _____
The **Mini Goal** that I will work on this week is: _____

_____

Why is this **Mini Goal** important to your goal process?_____

_____

The habit that I would like to focus on to support my goal this week is: _____

Action Steps that I can do to work toward my goal this week are:

_____   _____

_____   _____

_____   _____

*Plan out and list your **Action Steps** and habit goals on the line for each day on the following page. As you complete these tasks, check them off!*

NEW WEEK + NEW FOCUS = NEW YOU:

My **Primary Goal** is: _____

It is important that I reach this goal because: _____

_____

_____

Each day list three things that make you feel grateful.

MONTH / DAY	1 _____
	2 _____
	3 _____

Action Step _____ Complete ❑

Habit goal _____ Complete ❑

Notes _____

MONTH / DAY	1 _____
	2 _____
	3 _____

Action Step _____ Complete ❑

Habit goal _____ Complete ❑

Notes _____

MONTH / DAY	1 _____
	2 _____
	3 _____

Action Step _____ Complete ❑

Habit goal _____ Complete ❑

Notes _____

```
┌─────────┐
│ MONTH ╱ │   1 _____
│      ╱  │   2 _____
│    ╱ DAY│   3 _____
└─────────┘
```

Action Step _____ Complete ❏

Habit goal _____ Complete ❏

Notes _____

```
┌─────────┐
│ MONTH ╱ │   1 _____
│      ╱  │   2 _____
│    ╱ DAY│   3 _____
└─────────┘
```

Action Step _____ Complete ❏

Habit goal _____ Complete ❏

Notes _____

```
┌─────────┐
│ MONTH ╱ │   1 _____
│      ╱  │   2 _____
│    ╱ DAY│   3 _____
└─────────┘
```

Action Step _____ Complete ❏

Habit goal _____ Complete ❏

Notes _____

```
┌─────────┐
│ MONTH ╱ │   1 _____
│      ╱  │   2 _____
│    ╱ DAY│   3 _____
└─────────┘
```

Action Step _____ Complete ❏

Habit goal _____ Complete ❏

Notes _____

WEEKLY RECAP – GOALS:

Did you meet your **Mini Goal** for this week? ❏ Yes ❏ No
If no, do you need to spend another week on this **Mini Goal**
or would you prefer to move onto a new **Mini Goal** and return
to this **Mini Goal** another time? ❏ Same ❏ New
If you answered "Yes," which goal would you like to work on
this week?_____

What **Action Steps** helped the most toward achieving your
goal? _____

_____

Do you need to repeat any **Action Steps** to develop a habit?

_____

What did you notice and learn?_____

WEEKLY RECAP – GRATITUDE:

Without looking back at what you have written down during
the past week, answer the following questions:
What was the best part of your week?_____

_____

Who did you enjoy spending time with this week? _____

_____

Now look back at what you have written for the last week.
What do you notice about how you feel today versus how you
felt in the moment? _____

_____

Did any of these moments contribute to your **Primary Goal**? If
so, how? _____

_____

WEEKLY GOAL SETTING:

Refer to the previous page when completing this section.

If you did not meet your **Mini Goal**, what obstacles prevented you from doing so? _____

_____

_____

What **Action Steps** helped the most with your goal? Why?____

_____

_____

Do you need to repeat any **Action Steps** to help develop a habit? Which ones? _____

_____

What did you notice and learn?_____

_____

_____

My **Primary Goal** is: _____

The **Mini Goal** that I will work on this week is: _____

_____

Why is this **Mini Goal** important to your goal process?_____

_____

The habit that I would like to focus on to support my goal this week is: _____

Action Steps that I can do to work toward my goal this week are:

_____   _____

_____   _____

_____   _____

Plan out and list your **Action Steps** *and habit goals on the line for each day on the following page. As you complete these tasks, check them off!*

NEW WEEK + NEW FOCUS = NEW YOU:

My **Primary Goal** is: _____

It is important that I reach this goal because: _____

_____

_____

Each day list three things that make you feel grateful.

MONTH / DAY	1 _____
	2 _____
	3 _____

Action Step _____ Complete ❏

Habit goal _____ Complete ❏

Notes _____

MONTH / DAY	1 _____
	2 _____
	3 _____

Action Step _____ Complete ❏

Habit goal _____ Complete ❏

Notes _____

MONTH / DAY	1 _____
	2 _____
	3 _____

Action Step _____ Complete ❏

Habit goal _____ Complete ❏

Notes _____

MONTH
DAY

1 _____
2 _____
3 _____

Action Step _____ Complete ❑

Habit goal   _____ Complete ❑

Notes _____

MONTH
DAY

1 _____
2 _____
3 _____

Action Step _____ Complete ❑

Habit goal   _____ Complete ❑

Notes _____

MONTH
DAY

1 _____
2 _____
3 _____

Action Step _____ Complete ❑

Habit goal   _____ Complete ❑

Notes _____

MONTH
DAY

1 _____
2 _____
3 _____

Action Step _____ Complete ❑

Habit goal   _____ Complete ❑

Notes _____

WEEKLY RECAP – GOALS:

Did you meet your **Mini Goal** for this week? ❑ Yes ❑ No

If no, do you need to spend another week on this **Mini Goal** or would you prefer to move onto a new **Mini Goal** and return to this **Mini Goal** another time? ❑ Same ❑ New

If you answered "Yes," which goal would you like to work on this week?_____

What **Action Steps** helped the most toward achieving your goal? _____

_____

Do you need to repeat any **Action Steps** to develop a habit?

_____

What did you notice and learn?_____

_____

WEEKLY RECAP – GRATITUDE:

Without looking back at what you have written down during the past week, answer the following questions:

What was the best part of your week?_____

_____

Who did you enjoy spending time with this week? _____

_____

Now look back at what you have written for the last week. What do you notice about how you feel today versus how you felt in the moment? _____

_____

Did any of these moments contribute to your **Primary Goal**? If so, how? _____

_____

WEEKLY GOAL SETTING:

Refer to the previous page when completing this section.
If you did not meet your **Mini Goal**, what obstacles prevented you from doing so? _____

_____

_____

What **Action Steps** helped the most with your goal? Why?____

_____

_____

Do you need to repeat any **Action Steps** to help develop a habit? Which ones? _____

_____

What did you notice and learn?_____

_____

_____

My **Primary Goal** is: _____

The **Mini Goal** that I will work on this week is: _____

_____

Why is this **Mini Goal** important to your goal process?_____

_____

The habit that I would like to focus on to support my goal this week is: _____

Action Steps that I can do to work toward my goal this week are:

_____   _____

_____   _____

_____   _____

Plan out and list your **Action Steps** *and habit goals on the line for each day on the following page. As you complete these tasks, check them off!*

NEW WEEK + NEW FOCUS = NEW YOU:

My **Primary Goal** is: _____

It is important that I reach this goal because: _____

_____

_____

Each day list three things that make you feel grateful.

MONTH / DAY

1 _____

2 _____

3 _____

Action Step _____ Complete ❏

Habit goal _____ Complete ❏

Notes _____

MONTH / DAY

1 _____

2 _____

3 _____

Action Step _____ Complete ❏

Habit goal _____ Complete ❏

Notes _____

MONTH / DAY

1 _____

2 _____

3 _____

Action Step _____ Complete ❏

Habit goal _____ Complete ❏

Notes _____

MONTH / DAY

1 _____
2 _____
3 _____

Action Step _____ Complete ❑
Habit goal _____ Complete ❑
Notes _____

MONTH / DAY

1 _____
2 _____
3 _____

Action Step _____ Complete ❑
Habit goal _____ Complete ❑
Notes _____

MONTH / DAY

1 _____
2 _____
3 _____

Action Step _____ Complete ❑
Habit goal _____ Complete ❑
Notes _____

MONTH / DAY

1 _____
2 _____
3 _____

Action Step _____ Complete ❑
Habit goal _____ Complete ❑
Notes _____

WEEKLY RECAP – GOALS:

Did you meet your **Mini Goal** for this week? ❏ Yes ❏ No

If no, do you need to spend another week on this **Mini Goal** or would you prefer to move onto a new **Mini Goal** and return to this **Mini Goal** another time? ❏ Same ❏ New

If you answered "Yes," which goal would you like to work on this week?_____

What **Action Steps** helped the most toward achieving your goal? _____

_____

Do you need to repeat any **Action Steps** to develop a habit?

_____

What did you notice and learn?_____

WEEKLY RECAP – GRATITUDE:

Without looking back at what you have written down during the past week, answer the following questions:

What was the best part of your week?_____

_____

Who did you enjoy spending time with this week? _____

_____

Now look back at what you have written for the last week.

What do you notice about how you feel today versus how you felt in the moment? _____

_____

Did any of these moments contribute to your **Primary Goal**? If so, how? _____

_____

WEEKLY GOAL SETTING:

Refer to the previous page when completing this section.

If you did not meet your **Mini Goal**, what obstacles prevented you from doing so? _____

_____

_____

What **Action Steps** helped the most with your goal? Why?____

_____

_____

Do you need to repeat any **Action Steps** to help develop a habit? Which ones? _____

_____

What did you notice and learn? _____

_____

_____

My **Primary Goal** is: _____

The **Mini Goal** that I will work on this week is: _____

_____

Why is this **Mini Goal** important to your goal process? _____

_____

The habit that I would like to focus on to support my goal this week is: _____

Action Steps that I can do to work toward my goal this week are:

_____   _____

_____   _____

_____   _____

Plan out and list your **Action Steps** *and habit goals on the line for each day on the following page. As you complete these tasks, check them off!*

NEW WEEK + NEW FOCUS = NEW YOU:

My **Primary Goal** is: _____

It is important that I reach this goal because: _____

_____

_____

Each day list three things that make you feel grateful.

| MONTH / DAY | 1 _____ |
| 2 _____ |
| 3 _____ |

Action Step _____ Complete ❑

Habit goal _____ Complete ❑

Notes _____

| MONTH / DAY | 1 _____ |
| 2 _____ |
| 3 _____ |

Action Step _____ Complete ❑

Habit goal _____ Complete ❑

Notes _____

| MONTH / DAY | 1 _____ |
| 2 _____ |
| 3 _____ |

Action Step _____ Complete ❑

Habit goal _____ Complete ❑

Notes _____

```
MONTH
     /
    /
   /
      DAY
```
1 _____
2 _____
3 _____

Action Step _____ Complete ❏

Habit goal _____ Complete ❏

Notes _____

```
MONTH
     /
    /
   /
      DAY
```
1 _____
2 _____
3 _____

Action Step _____ Complete ❏

Habit goal _____ Complete ❏

Notes _____

```
MONTH
     /
    /
   /
      DAY
```
1 _____
2 _____
3 _____

Action Step _____ Complete ❏

Habit goal _____ Complete ❏

Notes _____

```
MONTH
     /
    /
   /
      DAY
```
1 _____
2 _____
3 _____

Action Step _____ Complete ❏

Habit goal _____ Complete ❏

Notes _____

WEEKLY RECAP – GOALS:

Did you meet your **Mini Goal** for this week? ❑ Yes ❑ No

If no, do you need to spend another week on this **Mini Goal** or would you prefer to move onto a new **Mini Goal** and return to this **Mini Goal** another time? ❑ Same ❑ New

If you answered "Yes," which goal would you like to work on this week?_____

What **Action Steps** helped the most toward achieving your goal? _____

_____

Do you need to repeat any **Action Steps** to develop a habit?

_____

What did you notice and learn?_____

_____

WEEKLY RECAP – GRATITUDE:

Without looking back at what you have written down during the past week, answer the following questions:

What was the best part of your week? _____

_____

Who did you enjoy spending time with this week? _____

_____

Now look back at what you have written for the last week.

What do you notice about how you feel today versus how you felt in the moment? _____

_____

Did any of these moments contribute to your **Primary Goal**? If so, how? _____

_____

WEEKLY GOAL SETTING:

Refer to the previous page when completing this section.

If you did not meet your **Mini Goal**, what obstacles prevented you from doing so? _____

_____

_____

What **Action Steps** helped the most with your goal? Why?_____

_____

_____

Do you need to repeat any **Action Steps** to help develop a habit? Which ones? _____

_____

What did you notice and learn?_____

_____

_____

My **Primary Goal** is: _____

The **Mini Goal** that I will work on this week is: _____

_____

Why is this **Mini Goal** important to your goal process?_____

_____

The habit that I would like to focus on to support my goal this week is: _____

Action Steps that I can do to work toward my goal this week are:

_____   _____

_____   _____

_____   _____

Plan out and list your **Action Steps** *and habit goals on the line for each day on the following page. As you complete these tasks, check them off!*

NEW WEEK + NEW FOCUS = NEW YOU:

My **Primary Goal** is: _____

It is important that I reach this goal because: _____

_____

_____

Each day list three things that make you feel grateful.

MONTH / DAY	1 _____
	2 _____
	3 _____

Action Step _____ Complete ❏

Habit goal _____ Complete ❏

Notes _____

MONTH / DAY	1 _____
	2 _____
	3 _____

Action Step _____ Complete ❏

Habit goal _____ Complete ❏

Notes _____

MONTH / DAY	1 _____
	2 _____
	3 _____

Action Step _____ Complete ❏

Habit goal _____ Complete ❏

Notes _____

MONTH	1 _____
DAY	2 _____
	3 _____

Action Step _____ Complete ❏

Habit goal _____ Complete ❏

Notes _____

MONTH	1 _____
DAY	2 _____
	3 _____

Action Step _____ Complete ❏

Habit goal _____ Complete ❏

Notes _____

MONTH	1 _____
DAY	2 _____
	3 _____

Action Step _____ Complete ❏

Habit goal _____ Complete ❏

Notes _____

MONTH	1 _____
DAY	2 _____
	3 _____

Action Step _____ Complete ❏

Habit goal _____ Complete ❏

Notes _____

WEEKLY RECAP – GOALS:

Did you meet your **Mini Goal** for this week? ❑ Yes ❑ No
If no, do you need to spend another week on this **Mini Goal**
or would you prefer to move onto a new **Mini Goal** and return
to this **Mini Goal** another time? ❑ Same ❑ New
If you answered "Yes," which goal would you like to work on
this week?_____
What **Action Steps** helped the most toward achieving your
goal? _____
_____
Do you need to repeat any **Action Steps** to develop a habit?
_____
What did you notice and learn?_____
_____

WEEKLY RECAP – GRATITUDE:

Without looking back at what you have written down during
the past week, answer the following questions:
What was the best part of your week? _____
_____
Who did you enjoy spending time with this week? _____
_____
Now look back at what you have written for the last week.
What do you notice about how you feel today versus how you
felt in the moment? _____
_____
Did any of these moments contribute to your **Primary Goal**? If
so, how? _____
_____

WEEKLY GOAL SETTING:

Refer to the previous page when completing this section.

If you did not meet your **Mini Goal**, what obstacles prevented you from doing so? _____

_____

_____

What **Action Steps** helped the most with your goal? Why?____

_____

_____

Do you need to repeat any **Action Steps** to help develop a habit? Which ones? _____

_____

What did you notice and learn?_____

_____

_____

My **Primary Goal** is: _____

The **Mini Goal** that I will work on this week is: _____

_____

Why is this **Mini Goal** important to your goal process?_____

_____

The habit that I would like to focus on to support my goal this week is: _____

Action Steps that I can do to work toward my goal this week are:

_____   _____

_____   _____

_____   _____

Plan out and list your **Action Steps** *and habit goals on the line for each day on the following page. As you complete these tasks, check them off!*

NEW WEEK + NEW FOCUS = NEW YOU:

My **Primary Goal** is: _____

It is important that I reach this goal because: _____

_____

_____

Each day list three things that make you feel grateful.

MONTH / DAY	1 _____
	2 _____
	3 _____

Action Step _____ Complete ❑

Habit goal _____ Complete ❑

Notes _____

MONTH / DAY	1 _____
	2 _____
	3 _____

Action Step _____ Complete ❑

Habit goal _____ Complete ❑

Notes _____

MONTH / DAY	1 _____
	2 _____
	3 _____

Action Step _____ Complete ❑

Habit goal _____ Complete ❑

Notes _____

MONTH / DAY	1 _____
	2 _____
	3 _____

Action Step _____ Complete ❏

Habit goal _____ Complete ❏

Notes _____

MONTH / DAY	1 _____
	2 _____
	3 _____

Action Step _____ Complete ❏

Habit goal _____ Complete ❏

Notes _____

MONTH / DAY	1 _____
	2 _____
	3 _____

Action Step _____ Complete ❏

Habit goal _____ Complete ❏

Notes _____

MONTH / DAY	1 _____
	2 _____
	3 _____

Action Step _____ Complete ❏

Habit goal _____ Complete ❏

Notes _____

WEEKLY RECAP – GOALS:

Did you meet your **Mini Goal** for this week? ❑ Yes ❑ No
If no, do you need to spend another week on this **Mini Goal**
or would you prefer to move onto a new **Mini Goal** and return
to this **Mini Goal** another time? ❑ Same ❑ New
If you answered "Yes," which goal would you like to work on
this week?_____
What **Action Steps** helped the most toward achieving your
goal? _____

_____
Do you need to repeat any **Action Steps** to develop a habit?

_____
What did you notice and learn?_____

_____

WEEKLY RECAP – GRATITUDE:

Without looking back at what you have written down during
the past week, answer the following questions:
What was the best part of your week?_____

_____
Who did you enjoy spending time with this week? _____

_____
Now look back at what you have written for the last week.
What do you notice about how you feel today versus how you
felt in the moment? _____

_____
Did any of these moments contribute to your **Primary Goal**? If
so, how? _____

_____

WEEKLY GOAL SETTING:

Refer to the previous page when completing this section.

If you did not meet your **Mini Goal**, what obstacles prevented you from doing so? _____

_____

_____

What **Action Steps** helped the most with your goal? Why?____

_____

_____

Do you need to repeat any **Action Steps** to help develop a habit? Which ones? _____

_____

What did you notice and learn?_____

_____

_____

My **Primary Goal** is: _____

The **Mini Goal** that I will work on this week is: _____

_____

Why is this **Mini Goal** important to your goal process?_____

_____

The habit that I would like to focus on to support my goal this week is: _____

Action Steps that I can do to work toward my goal this week are:

_____   _____

_____   _____

_____   _____

Plan out and list your **Action Steps** *and habit goals on the line for each day on the following page. As you complete these tasks, check them off!*

NEW WEEK + NEW FOCUS = NEW YOU:

My **Primary Goal** is: _____

It is important that I reach this goal because: _____

_____

_____

Each day list three things that make you feel grateful.

MONTH / DAY	1 _____
	2 _____
	3 _____

Action Step _____ Complete ❑

Habit goal   _____ Complete ❑

Notes _____

MONTH / DAY	1 _____
	2 _____
	3 _____

Action Step _____ Complete ❑

Habit goal   _____ Complete ❑

Notes _____

MONTH / DAY	1 _____
	2 _____
	3 _____

Action Step _____ Complete ❑

Habit goal   _____ Complete ❑

Notes _____

MONTH / DAY	1 _____
	2 _____
	3 _____

Action Step _____ Complete ❑

Habit goal _____ Complete ❑

Notes _____

MONTH / DAY	1 _____
	2 _____
	3 _____

Action Step _____ Complete ❑

Habit goal _____ Complete ❑

Notes _____

MONTH / DAY	1 _____
	2 _____
	3 _____

Action Step _____ Complete ❑

Habit goal _____ Complete ❑

Notes _____

MONTH / DAY	1 _____
	2 _____
	3 _____

Action Step _____ Complete ❑

Habit goal _____ Complete ❑

Notes _____

WEEKLY RECAP – GOALS:

Did you meet your **Mini Goal** for this week? ❏ Yes ❏ No

If no, do you need to spend another week on this **Mini Goal** or would you prefer to move onto a new **Mini Goal** and return to this **Mini Goal** another time? ❏ Same ❏ New

If you answered "Yes," which goal would you like to work on this week?_____

What **Action Steps** helped the most toward achieving your goal? _____

_____

Do you need to repeat any **Action Steps** to develop a habit?

_____

What did you notice and learn?_____

WEEKLY RECAP – GRATITUDE:

Without looking back at what you have written down during the past week, answer the following questions:

What was the best part of your week? _____

_____

Who did you enjoy spending time with this week? _____

_____

Now look back at what you have written for the last week.

What do you notice about how you feel today versus how you felt in the moment? _____

_____

Did any of these moments contribute to your **Primary Goal**? If so, how? _____

_____

WEEKLY GOAL SETTING:

Refer to the previous page when completing this section.
If you did not meet your **Mini Goal**, what obstacles prevented you from doing so? _____

_____

_____

What **Action Steps** helped the most with your goal? Why?____

_____

_____

Do you need to repeat any **Action Steps** to help develop a habit? Which ones? _____

_____

What did you notice and learn?_____

_____

_____

My **Primary Goal** is: _____

The **Mini Goal** that I will work on this week is: _____

_____

Why is this **Mini Goal** important to your goal process?_____

_____

The habit that I would like to focus on to support my goal this week is: _____

Action Steps that I can do to work toward my goal this week are:

_____   _____

_____   _____

_____   _____

Plan out and list your **Action Steps** *and habit goals on the line for each day on the following page. As you complete these tasks, check them off!*

NEW WEEK + NEW FOCUS = NEW YOU:

My **Primary Goal** is: _____

It is important that I reach this goal because: _____

_____

_____

Each day list three things that make you feel grateful.

MONTH / DAY

1 _____

2 _____

3 _____

Action Step _____ Complete ❑

Habit goal _____ Complete ❑

Notes _____

MONTH / DAY

1 _____

2 _____

3 _____

Action Step _____ Complete ❑

Habit goal _____ Complete ❑

Notes _____

MONTH / DAY

1 _____

2 _____

3 _____

Action Step _____ Complete ❑

Habit goal _____ Complete ❑

Notes _____

MONTH / DAY	1 _____
	2 _____
	3 _____

Action Step _____ Complete ❑

Habit goal _____ Complete ❑

Notes _____

MONTH / DAY	1 _____
	2 _____
	3 _____

Action Step _____ Complete ❑

Habit goal _____ Complete ❑

Notes _____

MONTH / DAY	1 _____
	2 _____
	3 _____

Action Step _____ Complete ❑

Habit goal _____ Complete ❑

Notes _____

MONTH / DAY	1 _____
	2 _____
	3 _____

Action Step _____ Complete ❑

Habit goal _____ Complete ❑

Notes _____

WEEKLY RECAP – GOALS:

Did you meet your **Mini Goal** for this week? ❏ Yes ❏ No
If no, do you need to spend another week on this **Mini Goal** or would you prefer to move onto a new **Mini Goal** and return to this **Mini Goal** another time? ❏ Same ❏ New
If you answered "Yes," which goal would you like to work on this week?_____

What **Action Steps** helped the most toward achieving your goal? _____

_____

Do you need to repeat any **Action Steps** to develop a habit?

_____

What did you notice and learn?_____

WEEKLY RECAP – GRATITUDE:

Without looking back at what you have written down during the past week, answer the following questions:
What was the best part of your week? _____

_____

Who did you enjoy spending time with this week? _____

_____

Now look back at what you have written for the last week. What do you notice about how you feel today versus how you felt in the moment? _____

_____

Did any of these moments contribute to your **Primary Goal**? If so, how? _____

_____

WEEKLY GOAL SETTING:

Refer to the previous page when completing this section.

If you did not meet your **Mini Goal**, what obstacles prevented you from doing so? _____

_____

_____

What **Action Steps** helped the most with your goal? Why?____

_____

_____

Do you need to repeat any **Action Steps** to help develop a habit? Which ones? _____

_____

What did you notice and learn?_____

_____

_____

My **Primary Goal** is: _____

The **Mini Goal** that I will work on this week is: _____

_____

Why is this **Mini Goal** important to your goal process?_____

_____

The habit that I would like to focus on to support my goal this week is: _____

Action Steps that I can do to work toward my goal this week are:

_____   _____

_____   _____

_____   _____

Plan out and list your **Action Steps** *and habit goals on the line for each day on the following page. As you complete these tasks, check them off!*

NEW WEEK + NEW FOCUS = NEW YOU:

My **Primary Goal** is: _____

It is important that I reach this goal because: _____

_____

_____

Each day list three things that make you feel grateful.

MONTH / DAY	1 _____
	2 _____
	3 _____

Action Step _____ Complete ❏

Habit goal _____ Complete ❏

Notes _____

MONTH / DAY	1 _____
	2 _____
	3 _____

Action Step _____ Complete ❏

Habit goal _____ Complete ❏

Notes _____

MONTH / DAY	1 _____
	2 _____
	3 _____

Action Step _____ Complete ❏

Habit goal _____ Complete ❏

Notes _____

MONTH / DAY	1 _____
	2 _____
	3 _____

Action Step _____ Complete ❏

Habit goal _____ Complete ❏

Notes _____

MONTH / DAY	1 _____
	2 _____
	3 _____

Action Step _____ Complete ❏

Habit goal _____ Complete ❏

Notes _____

MONTH / DAY	1 _____
	2 _____
	3 _____

Action Step _____ Complete ❏

Habit goal _____ Complete ❏

Notes _____

MONTH / DAY	1 _____
	2 _____
	3 _____

Action Step _____ Complete ❏

Habit goal _____ Complete ❏

Notes _____

WEEKLY RECAP – GOALS:

Did you meet your **Mini Goal** for this week? ❏ Yes ❏ No
If no, do you need to spend another week on this **Mini Goal**
or would you prefer to move onto a new **Mini Goal** and return
to this **Mini Goal** another time? ❏ Same ❏ New
If you answered "Yes," which goal would you like to work on
this week?_____
What **Action Steps** helped the most toward achieving your
goal? _____
_____
Do you need to repeat any **Action Steps** to develop a habit?
_____
What did you notice and learn?_____
_____

WEEKLY RECAP – GRATITUDE:

Without looking back at what you have written down during
the past week, answer the following questions:
What was the best part of your week?_____
_____
Who did you enjoy spending time with this week? _____
_____
Now look back at what you have written for the last week.
What do you notice about how you feel today versus how you
felt in the moment? _____
_____
Did any of these moments contribute to your **Primary Goal**? If
so, how? _____
_____

WEEKLY GOAL SETTING:

Refer to the previous page when completing this section.

If you did not meet your **Mini Goal**, what obstacles prevented you from doing so? _____

_____

_____

What **Action Steps** helped the most with your goal? Why?____

_____

_____

Do you need to repeat any **Action Steps** to help develop a habit? Which ones? _____

_____

What did you notice and learn?_____

_____

_____

My **Primary Goal** is: _____

The **Mini Goal** that I will work on this week is: _____

_____

Why is this **Mini Goal** important to your goal process?_____

_____

The habit that I would like to focus on to support my goal this week is: _____

Action Steps that I can do to work toward my goal this week are:

_____   _____

_____   _____

_____   _____

*Plan out and list your **Action Steps** and habit goals on the line for each day on the following page. As you complete these tasks, check them off!*

NEW WEEK + NEW FOCUS = NEW YOU:

My **Primary Goal** is: _____

It is important that I reach this goal because: _____

_____

_____

Each day list three things that make you feel grateful.

MONTH / DAY	
	1 _____
	2 _____
	3 _____

Action Step _____ Complete ❑

Habit goal   _____ Complete ❑

Notes _____

MONTH / DAY	
	1 _____
	2 _____
	3 _____

Action Step _____ Complete ❑

Habit goal   _____ Complete ❑

Notes _____

MONTH / DAY	
	1 _____
	2 _____
	3 _____

Action Step _____ Complete ❑

Habit goal   _____ Complete ❑

Notes _____

MONTH / DAY	1 _____
	2 _____
	3 _____

Action Step _____ Complete ❑

Habit goal _____ Complete ❑

Notes _____

MONTH / DAY	1 _____
	2 _____
	3 _____

Action Step _____ Complete ❑

Habit goal _____ Complete ❑

Notes _____

MONTH / DAY	1 _____
	2 _____
	3 _____

Action Step _____ Complete ❑

Habit goal _____ Complete ❑

Notes _____

MONTH / DAY	1 _____
	2 _____
	3 _____

Action Step _____ Complete ❑

Habit goal _____ Complete ❑

Notes _____

WEEKLY RECAP – GOALS:

Did you meet your **Mini Goal** for this week? ❏ Yes ❏ No

If no, do you need to spend another week on this **Mini Goal** or would you prefer to move onto a new **Mini Goal** and return to this **Mini Goal** another time? ❏ Same ❏ New

If you answered "Yes," which goal would you like to work on this week?_____

What **Action Steps** helped the most toward achieving your goal? _____

_____

Do you need to repeat any **Action Steps** to develop a habit?

_____

What did you notice and learn?_____

WEEKLY RECAP – GRATITUDE:

Without looking back at what you have written down during the past week, answer the following questions:

What was the best part of your week?_____

_____

Who did you enjoy spending time with this week? _____

_____

Now look back at what you have written for the last week.

What do you notice about how you feel today versus how you felt in the moment? _____

_____

Did any of these moments contribute to your **Primary Goal**? If so, how? _____

_____

WEEKLY GOAL SETTING:

Refer to the previous page when completing this section.

If you did not meet your **Mini Goal**, what obstacles prevented you from doing so? _____

_____

_____

What **Action Steps** helped the most with your goal? Why?____

_____

_____

Do you need to repeat any **Action Steps** to help develop a habit? Which ones? _____

_____

What did you notice and learn?_____

_____

_____

My **Primary Goal** is: _____

The **Mini Goal** that I will work on this week is: _____

_____

Why is this **Mini Goal** important to your goal process?_____

_____

The habit that I would like to focus on to support my goal this week is: _____

Action Steps that I can do to work toward my goal this week are:

_____   _____

_____   _____

_____   _____

*Plan out and list your **Action Steps** and habit goals on the line for each day on the following page. As you complete these tasks, check them off!*

NEW WEEK + NEW FOCUS = NEW YOU:

My **Primary Goal** is: _____

It is important that I reach this goal because: _____

_____

_____

Each day list three things that make you feel grateful.

MONTH / DAY	1 _____
	2 _____
	3 _____

Action Step _____ Complete ❏

Habit goal _____ Complete ❏

Notes _____

MONTH / DAY	1 _____
	2 _____
	3 _____

Action Step _____ Complete ❏

Habit goal _____ Complete ❏

Notes _____

MONTH / DAY	1 _____
	2 _____
	3 _____

Action Step _____ Complete ❏

Habit goal _____ Complete ❏

Notes _____

MONTH / DAY

1 _____
2 _____
3 _____

Action Step _____ Complete ❏

Habit goal _____ Complete ❏

Notes _____

MONTH / DAY

1 _____
2 _____
3 _____

Action Step _____ Complete ❏

Habit goal _____ Complete ❏

Notes _____

MONTH / DAY

1 _____
2 _____
3 _____

Action Step _____ Complete ❏

Habit goal _____ Complete ❏

Notes _____

MONTH / DAY

1 _____
2 _____
3 _____

Action Step _____ Complete ❏

Habit goal _____ Complete ❏

Notes _____

WEEKLY RECAP – GOALS:

Did you meet your **Mini Goal** for this week? ❑ Yes ❑ No
If no, do you need to spend another week on this **Mini Goal**
or would you prefer to move onto a new **Mini Goal** and return
to this **Mini Goal** another time? ❑ Same ❑ New
If you answered "Yes," which goal would you like to work on
this week?_____
What **Action Steps** helped the most toward achieving your
goal? _____

_____

Do you need to repeat any **Action Steps** to develop a habit?

_____

What did you notice and learn?_____

_____

WEEKLY RECAP – GRATITUDE:

Without looking back at what you have written down during
the past week, answer the following questions:
What was the best part of your week? _____

_____

Who did you enjoy spending time with this week? _____

_____

Now look back at what you have written for the last week.
What do you notice about how you feel today versus how you
felt in the moment? _____

_____

Did any of these moments contribute to your **Primary Goal**? If
so, how? _____

_____

WEEKLY GOAL SETTING:

Refer to the previous page when completing this section.

If you did not meet your **Mini Goal**, what obstacles prevented you from doing so? _____

_____

_____

What **Action Steps** helped the most with your goal? Why?____

_____

_____

Do you need to repeat any **Action Steps** to help develop a habit? Which ones? _____

_____

What did you notice and learn?_____

_____

_____

My **Primary Goal** is: _____

The **Mini Goal** that I will work on this week is: _____

_____

Why is this **Mini Goal** important to your goal process?_____

_____

The habit that I would like to focus on to support my goal this week is: _____

Action Steps that I can do to work toward my goal this week are:

_____   _____

_____   _____

_____   _____

Plan out and list your **Action Steps** *and habit goals on the line for each day on the following page. As you complete these tasks, check them off!*

NEW WEEK + NEW FOCUS = NEW YOU:

My **Primary Goal** is: _____

It is important that I reach this goal because: _____

_____

_____

Each day list three things that make you feel grateful.

MONTH / DAY	1 _____
	2 _____
	3 _____

Action Step _____ Complete ❏

Habit goal   _____ Complete ❏

Notes _____

MONTH / DAY	1 _____
	2 _____
	3 _____

Action Step _____ Complete ❏

Habit goal   _____ Complete ❏

Notes _____

MONTH / DAY	1 _____
	2 _____
	3 _____

Action Step _____ Complete ❏

Habit goal   _____ Complete ❏

Notes _____

MONTH / DAY

1 _____
2 _____
3 _____

Action Step _____ Complete ❏

Habit goal _____ Complete ❏

Notes _____

MONTH / DAY

1 _____
2 _____
3 _____

Action Step _____ Complete ❏

Habit goal _____ Complete ❏

Notes _____

MONTH / DAY

1 _____
2 _____
3 _____

Action Step _____ Complete ❏

Habit goal _____ Complete ❏

Notes _____

MONTH / DAY

1 _____
2 _____
3 _____

Action Step _____ Complete ❏

Habit goal _____ Complete ❏

Notes _____

WEEKLY RECAP – GOALS:

Did you meet your **Mini Goal** for this week? ❏ Yes ❏ No
If no, do you need to spend another week on this **Mini Goal**
or would you prefer to move onto a new **Mini Goal** and return
to this **Mini Goal** another time? ❏ Same ❏ New
If you answered "Yes," which goal would you like to work on
this week?_____
What **Action Steps** helped the most toward achieving your
goal? _____
_____
Do you need to repeat any **Action Steps** to develop a habit?
_____
What did you notice and learn?_____
_____

WEEKLY RECAP – GRATITUDE:

Without looking back at what you have written down during
the past week, answer the following questions:
What was the best part of your week?_____
_____
Who did you enjoy spending time with this week? _____
_____
Now look back at what you have written for the last week.
What do you notice about how you feel today versus how you
felt in the moment? _____
_____
Did any of these moments contribute to your **Primary Goal**? If
so, how? _____
_____

WEEKLY GOAL SETTING:

Refer to the previous page when completing this section.
If you did not meet your **Mini Goal**, what obstacles prevented you from doing so? _____

_____

_____

What **Action Steps** helped the most with your goal? Why?____

_____

_____

Do you need to repeat any **Action Steps** to help develop a habit? Which ones? _____

_____

What did you notice and learn?_____

_____

_____

My **Primary Goal** is: _____

The **Mini Goal** that I will work on this week is: _____

_____

Why is this **Mini Goal** important to your goal process?_____

_____

The habit that I would like to focus on to support my goal this week is: _____

Action Steps that I can do to work toward my goal this week are:

_____   _____

_____   _____

_____   _____

Plan out and list your **Action Steps** *and habit goals on the line for each day on the following page. As you complete these tasks, check them off!*

NEW WEEK + NEW FOCUS = NEW YOU:

My **Primary Goal** is: _____

It is important that I reach this goal because: _____

_____

_____

Each day list three things that make you feel grateful.

MONTH / DAY	1 _____
	2 _____
	3 _____

Action Step _____ Complete ❏

Habit goal _____ Complete ❏

Notes _____

MONTH / DAY	1 _____
	2 _____
	3 _____

Action Step _____ Complete ❏

Habit goal _____ Complete ❏

Notes _____

MONTH / DAY	1 _____
	2 _____
	3 _____

Action Step _____ Complete ❏

Habit goal _____ Complete ❏

Notes _____

MONTH /
DAY

1 _____

2 _____

3 _____

Action Step _____ Complete ❏

Habit goal _____ Complete ❏

Notes _____

MONTH /
DAY

1 _____

2 _____

3 _____

Action Step _____ Complete ❏

Habit goal _____ Complete ❏

Notes _____

MONTH /
DAY

1 _____

2 _____

3 _____

Action Step _____ Complete ❏

Habit goal _____ Complete ❏

Notes _____

MONTH /
DAY

1 _____

2 _____

3 _____

Action Step _____ Complete ❏

Habit goal _____ Complete ❏

Notes _____

WEEKLY RECAP – GOALS:

Did you meet your **Mini Goal** for this week? ❑ Yes ❑ No
If no, do you need to spend another week on this **Mini Goal**
or would you prefer to move onto a new **Mini Goal** and return
to this **Mini Goal** another time? ❑ Same ❑ New
If you answered "Yes," which goal would you like to work on
this week?_____
What **Action Steps** helped the most toward achieving your
goal? _____

_____
Do you need to repeat any **Action Steps** to develop a habit?

_____
What did you notice and learn?_____

_____

WEEKLY RECAP – GRATITUDE:

Without looking back at what you have written down during
the past week, answer the following questions:
What was the best part of your week?_____

_____
Who did you enjoy spending time with this week? _____

_____
Now look back at what you have written for the last week.
What do you notice about how you feel today versus how you
felt in the moment? _____

_____
Did any of these moments contribute to your **Primary Goal**? If
so, how? _____

_____

WEEKLY GOAL SETTING:

Refer to the previous page when completing this section.
If you did not meet your **Mini Goal**, what obstacles prevented you from doing so? _____

_____
_____

What **Action Steps** helped the most with your goal? Why?____

_____
_____

Do you need to repeat any **Action Steps** to help develop a habit? Which ones? _____

_____

What did you notice and learn?_____

_____
_____

My **Primary Goal** is: _____
The **Mini Goal** that I will work on this week is: _____

_____

Why is this **Mini Goal** important to your goal process?_____

_____

The habit that I would like to focus on to support my goal this week is: _____

Action Steps that I can do to work toward my goal this week are:

_____   _____

_____   _____

_____   _____

*Plan out and list your **Action Steps** and habit goals on the line for each day on the following page. As you complete these tasks, check them off!*

NEW WEEK + NEW FOCUS = NEW YOU:

My **Primary Goal** is: _____

It is important that I reach this goal because: _____

_____

_____

Each day list three things that make you feel grateful.

MONTH / DAY	1 _____
	2 _____
	3 _____

Action Step _____ Complete ❏

Habit goal _____ Complete ❏

Notes _____

MONTH / DAY	1 _____
	2 _____
	3 _____

Action Step _____ Complete ❏

Habit goal _____ Complete ❏

Notes _____

MONTH / DAY	1 _____
	2 _____
	3 _____

Action Step _____ Complete ❏

Habit goal _____ Complete ❏

Notes _____

```
┌─────────┐
│ MONTH ╱ │   1 _____
│      ╱  │   2 _____
│    ╱ DAY│   3 _____
└─────────┘
```

Action Step _____ Complete ❑

Habit goal   _____ Complete ❑

Notes _____

```
┌─────────┐
│ MONTH ╱ │   1 _____
│      ╱  │   2 _____
│    ╱ DAY│   3 _____
└─────────┘
```

Action Step _____ Complete ❑

Habit goal   _____ Complete ❑

Notes _____

```
┌─────────┐
│ MONTH ╱ │   1 _____
│      ╱  │   2 _____
│    ╱ DAY│   3 _____
└─────────┘
```

Action Step _____ Complete ❑

Habit goal   _____ Complete ❑

Notes _____

```
┌─────────┐
│ MONTH ╱ │   1 _____
│      ╱  │   2 _____
│    ╱ DAY│   3 _____
└─────────┘
```

Action Step _____ Complete ❑

Habit goal   _____ Complete ❑

Notes _____

WEEKLY RECAP – GOALS:

Did you meet your **Mini Goal** for this week? ❑ Yes ❑ No

If no, do you need to spend another week on this **Mini Goal** or would you prefer to move onto a new **Mini Goal** and return to this **Mini Goal** another time? ❑ Same ❑ New

If you answered "Yes," which goal would you like to work on this week?_____

What **Action Steps** helped the most toward achieving your goal? _____

_____

Do you need to repeat any **Action Steps** to develop a habit?

_____

What did you notice and learn?_____

WEEKLY RECAP – GRATITUDE:

Without looking back at what you have written down during the past week, answer the following questions:

What was the best part of your week? _____

_____

Who did you enjoy spending time with this week? _____

_____

Now look back at what you have written for the last week. What do you notice about how you feel today versus how you felt in the moment? _____

_____

Did any of these moments contribute to your **Primary Goal**? If so, how? _____

_____

WEEKLY GOAL SETTING:

Refer to the previous page when completing this section.

If you did not meet your **Mini Goal**, what obstacles prevented you from doing so? _____

_____

_____

What **Action Steps** helped the most with your goal? Why?____

_____

_____

Do you need to repeat any **Action Steps** to help develop a habit? Which ones? _____

_____

What did you notice and learn?_____

_____

_____

My **Primary Goal** is: _____

The **Mini Goal** that I will work on this week is: _____

_____

Why is this **Mini Goal** important to your goal process?_____

_____

The habit that I would like to focus on to support my goal this week is: _____

Action Steps that I can do to work toward my goal this week are:

_____   _____

_____   _____

_____   _____

Plan out and list your **Action Steps** *and habit goals on the line for each day on the following page. As you complete these tasks, check them off!*

NEW WEEK + NEW FOCUS = NEW YOU:

My **Primary Goal** is: _____

It is important that I reach this goal because: _____

_____

_____

Each day list three things that make you feel grateful.

MONTH / DAY	1 _____
	2 _____
	3 _____

Action Step _____ Complete ❏

Habit goal _____ Complete ❏

Notes _____

MONTH / DAY	1 _____
	2 _____
	3 _____

Action Step _____ Complete ❏

Habit goal _____ Complete ❏

Notes _____

MONTH / DAY	1 _____
	2 _____
	3 _____

Action Step _____ Complete ❏

Habit goal _____ Complete ❏

Notes _____

MONTH / DAY	1 _____
	2 _____
	3 _____

Action Step _____ Complete ❏

Habit goal _____ Complete ❏

Notes _____

MONTH / DAY	1 _____
	2 _____
	3 _____

Action Step _____ Complete ❏

Habit goal _____ Complete ❏

Notes _____

MONTH / DAY	1 _____
	2 _____
	3 _____

Action Step _____ Complete ❏

Habit goal _____ Complete ❏

Notes _____

MONTH / DAY	1 _____
	2 _____
	3 _____

Action Step _____ Complete ❏

Habit goal _____ Complete ❏

Notes _____

WEEKLY RECAP – GOALS:

Did you meet your **Mini Goal** for this week? ❑ Yes ❑ No
If no, do you need to spend another week on this **Mini Goal**
or would you prefer to move onto a new **Mini Goal** and return
to this **Mini Goal** another time? ❑ Same ❑ New
If you answered "Yes," which goal would you like to work on
this week?_____
What **Action Steps** helped the most toward achieving your
goal? _____

_____

Do you need to repeat any **Action Steps** to develop a habit?

_____

What did you notice and learn?_____

WEEKLY RECAP – GRATITUDE:

Without looking back at what you have written down during
the past week, answer the following questions:
What was the best part of your week?_____

_____

Who did you enjoy spending time with this week? _____

_____

Now look back at what you have written for the last week.
What do you notice about how you feel today versus how you
felt in the moment? _____

_____

Did any of these moments contribute to your **Primary Goal**? If
so, how? _____

_____

WEEKLY GOAL SETTING:

Refer to the previous page when completing this section.

If you did not meet your **Mini Goal**, what obstacles prevented you from doing so? _____

_____

_____

What **Action Steps** helped the most with your goal? Why?____

_____

_____

Do you need to repeat any **Action Steps** to help develop a habit? Which ones? _____

_____

What did you notice and learn?_____

_____

_____

My **Primary Goal** is: _____

The **Mini Goal** that I will work on this week is: _____

_____

Why is this **Mini Goal** important to your goal process?_____

_____

The habit that I would like to focus on to support my goal this week is: _____

Action Steps that I can do to work toward my goal this week are:

_____   _____

_____   _____

_____   _____

Plan out and list your **Action Steps** *and habit goals on the line for each day on the following page. As you complete these tasks, check them off!*

NEW WEEK + NEW FOCUS = NEW YOU:

My **Primary Goal** is: _____

It is important that I reach this goal because: _____

_____

_____

Each day list three things that make you feel grateful.

MONTH / DAY	1 _____
	2 _____
	3 _____

Action Step _____ Complete ❏

Habit goal _____ Complete ❏

Notes _____

MONTH / DAY	1 _____
	2 _____
	3 _____

Action Step _____ Complete ❏

Habit goal _____ Complete ❏

Notes _____

MONTH / DAY	1 _____
	2 _____
	3 _____

Action Step _____ Complete ❏

Habit goal _____ Complete ❏

Notes _____

MONTH / DAY

1 _____
2 _____
3 _____

Action Step _____ Complete ❑

Habit goal _____ Complete ❑

Notes _____

MONTH / DAY

1 _____
2 _____
3 _____

Action Step _____ Complete ❑

Habit goal _____ Complete ❑

Notes _____

MONTH / DAY

1 _____
2 _____
3 _____

Action Step _____ Complete ❑

Habit goal _____ Complete ❑

Notes _____

MONTH / DAY

1 _____
2 _____
3 _____

Action Step _____ Complete ❑

Habit goal _____ Complete ❑

Notes _____

WEEKLY RECAP – GOALS:

Did you meet your **Mini Goal** for this week? ❏ Yes ❏ No
If no, do you need to spend another week on this **Mini Goal**
or would you prefer to move onto a new **Mini Goal** and return
to this **Mini Goal** another time? ❏ Same ❏ New
If you answered "Yes," which goal would you like to work on
this week?_____
What **Action Steps** helped the most toward achieving your
goal? _____
_____
Do you need to repeat any **Action Steps** to develop a habit?
_____
What did you notice and learn?_____

WEEKLY RECAP – GRATITUDE:

Without looking back at what you have written down during
the past week, answer the following questions:
What was the best part of your week? _____
_____
Who did you enjoy spending time with this week? _____
_____
Now look back at what you have written for the last week.
What do you notice about how you feel today versus how you
felt in the moment? _____
_____
Did any of these moments contribute to your **Primary Goal**? If
so, how? _____
_____

WEEKLY GOAL SETTING:

Refer to the previous page when completing this section.

If you did not meet your **Mini Goal**, what obstacles prevented you from doing so? _____

_____

_____

What **Action Steps** helped the most with your goal? Why?____

_____

_____

Do you need to repeat any **Action Steps** to help develop a habit? Which ones? _____

_____

What did you notice and learn?_____

_____

_____

My **Primary Goal** is: _____

The **Mini Goal** that I will work on this week is: _____

_____

Why is this **Mini Goal** important to your goal process?_____

_____

The habit that I would like to focus on to support my goal this week is: _____

Action Steps that I can do to work toward my goal this week are:

_____   _____

_____   _____

_____   _____

*Plan out and list your **Action Steps** and habit goals on the line for each day on the following page. As you complete these tasks, check them off!*

NEW WEEK + NEW FOCUS = NEW YOU:

My **Primary Goal** is: _____

It is important that I reach this goal because: _____

_____

_____

Each day list three things that make you feel grateful.

MONTH / DAY	1 _____
	2 _____
	3 _____

Action Step _____ Complete ❑

Habit goal _____ Complete ❑

Notes _____

MONTH / DAY	1 _____
	2 _____
	3 _____

Action Step _____ Complete ❑

Habit goal _____ Complete ❑

Notes _____

MONTH / DAY	1 _____
	2 _____
	3 _____

Action Step _____ Complete ❑

Habit goal _____ Complete ❑

Notes _____

MONTH / DAY

1 _____
2 _____
3 _____

Action Step _____ Complete ❑
Habit goal _____ Complete ❑
Notes _____

MONTH / DAY

1 _____
2 _____
3 _____

Action Step _____ Complete ❑
Habit goal _____ Complete ❑
Notes _____

MONTH / DAY

1 _____
2 _____
3 _____

Action Step _____ Complete ❑
Habit goal _____ Complete ❑
Notes _____

MONTH / DAY

1 _____
2 _____
3 _____

Action Step _____ Complete ❑
Habit goal _____ Complete ❑
Notes _____

WEEKLY RECAP – GOALS:

Did you meet your **Mini Goal** for this week? ❑ Yes ❑ No

If no, do you need to spend another week on this **Mini Goal** or would you prefer to move onto a new **Mini Goal** and return to this **Mini Goal** another time? ❑ Same ❑ New

If you answered "Yes," which goal would you like to work on this week?_____

What **Action Steps** helped the most toward achieving your goal? _____

_____

Do you need to repeat any **Action Steps** to develop a habit?

_____

What did you notice and learn?_____

WEEKLY RECAP – GRATITUDE:

Without looking back at what you have written down during the past week, answer the following questions:

What was the best part of your week? _____

_____

Who did you enjoy spending time with this week? _____

_____

Now look back at what you have written for the last week. What do you notice about how you feel today versus how you felt in the moment? _____

_____

Did any of these moments contribute to your **Primary Goal**? If so, how? _____

_____

WEEKLY GOAL SETTING:

Refer to the previous page when completing this section.

If you did not meet your **Mini Goal**, what obstacles prevented you from doing so? _____

_____

_____

What **Action Steps** helped the most with your goal? Why?____

_____

_____

Do you need to repeat any **Action Steps** to help develop a habit? Which ones? _____

_____

What did you notice and learn? _____

_____

_____

My **Primary Goal** is: _____

The **Mini Goal** that I will work on this week is: _____

_____

Why is this **Mini Goal** important to your goal process? _____

_____

The habit that I would like to focus on to support my goal this week is: _____

Action Steps that I can do to work toward my goal this week are:

_____   _____

_____   _____

_____   _____

*Plan out and list your **Action Steps** and habit goals on the line for each day on the following page. As you complete these tasks, check them off!*

NEW WEEK + NEW FOCUS = NEW YOU:

My **Primary Goal** is: _____

It is important that I reach this goal because: _____

_____

_____

Each day list three things that make you feel grateful.

MONTH / DAY	1 _____
	2 _____
	3 _____

Action Step _____ Complete ❏

Habit goal _____ Complete ❏

Notes _____

MONTH / DAY	1 _____
	2 _____
	3 _____

Action Step _____ Complete ❏

Habit goal _____ Complete ❏

Notes _____

MONTH / DAY	1 _____
	2 _____
	3 _____

Action Step _____ Complete ❏

Habit goal _____ Complete ❏

Notes _____

```
┌─────────┐
│ MONTH  ╱│   1 _____
│      ╱  │   2 _____
│    ╱    │   3 _____
│  ╱  DAY │
└─────────┘
```

Action Step _____ Complete ❏

Habit goal _____ Complete ❏

Notes _____

```
┌─────────┐
│ MONTH  ╱│   1 _____
│      ╱  │   2 _____
│    ╱    │   3 _____
│  ╱  DAY │
└─────────┘
```

Action Step _____ Complete ❏

Habit goal _____ Complete ❏

Notes _____

```
┌─────────┐
│ MONTH  ╱│   1 _____
│      ╱  │   2 _____
│    ╱    │   3 _____
│  ╱  DAY │
└─────────┘
```

Action Step _____ Complete ❏

Habit goal _____ Complete ❏

Notes _____

```
┌─────────┐
│ MONTH  ╱│   1 _____
│      ╱  │   2 _____
│    ╱    │   3 _____
│  ╱  DAY │
└─────────┘
```

Action Step _____ Complete ❏

Habit goal _____ Complete ❏

Notes _____

WEEKLY RECAP – GOALS:

Did you meet your **Mini Goal** for this week? ❑ Yes ❑ No
If no, do you need to spend another week on this **Mini Goal** or would you prefer to move onto a new **Mini Goal** and return to this **Mini Goal** another time? ❑ Same ❑ New
If you answered "Yes," which goal would you like to work on this week?_____
What **Action Steps** helped the most toward achieving your goal? _____

_____
Do you need to repeat any **Action Steps** to develop a habit?

_____
What did you notice and learn?_____

_____

WEEKLY RECAP – GRATITUDE:

Without looking back at what you have written down during the past week, answer the following questions:
What was the best part of your week?_____

_____
Who did you enjoy spending time with this week? _____

_____
Now look back at what you have written for the last week.
What do you notice about how you feel today versus how you felt in the moment? _____

_____
Did any of these moments contribute to your **Primary Goal**? If so, how? _____

_____

WEEKLY GOAL SETTING:

Refer to the previous page when completing this section.

If you did not meet your **Mini Goal**, what obstacles prevented you from doing so? _____

_____

_____

What **Action Steps** helped the most with your goal? Why?____

_____

_____

Do you need to repeat any **Action Steps** to help develop a habit? Which ones? _____

_____

What did you notice and learn?_____

_____

_____

My **Primary Goal** is: _____

The **Mini Goal** that I will work on this week is: _____

_____

Why is this **Mini Goal** important to your goal process?_____

_____

The habit that I would like to focus on to support my goal this week is: _____

Action Steps that I can do to work toward my goal this week are:

_____   _____

_____   _____

_____   _____

*Plan out and list your **Action Steps** and habit goals on the line for each day on the following page. As you complete these tasks, check them off!*

NEW WEEK + NEW FOCUS = NEW YOU:

My **Primary Goal** is: _____

It is important that I reach this goal because: _____

_____

_____

Each day list three things that make you feel grateful.

MONTH / DAY	1 _____
	2 _____
	3 _____

Action Step _____ Complete ❑

Habit goal   _____ Complete ❑

Notes _____

MONTH / DAY	1 _____
	2 _____
	3 _____

Action Step _____ Complete ❑

Habit goal   _____ Complete ❑

Notes _____

MONTH / DAY	1 _____
	2 _____
	3 _____

Action Step _____ Complete ❑

Habit goal   _____ Complete ❑

Notes _____

MONTH / DAY	1 _____
	2 _____
	3 _____

Action Step _____ Complete ❏

Habit goal _____ Complete ❏

Notes _____

MONTH / DAY	1 _____
	2 _____
	3 _____

Action Step _____ Complete ❏

Habit goal _____ Complete ❏

Notes _____

MONTH / DAY	1 _____
	2 _____
	3 _____

Action Step _____ Complete ❏

Habit goal _____ Complete ❏

Notes _____

MONTH / DAY	1 _____
	2 _____
	3 _____

Action Step _____ Complete ❏

Habit goal _____ Complete ❏

Notes _____

WEEKLY RECAP – GOALS:

Did you meet your **Mini Goal** for this week? ❏ Yes ❏ No

If no, do you need to spend another week on this **Mini Goal** or would you prefer to move onto a new **Mini Goal** and return to this **Mini Goal** another time? ❏ Same ❏ New

If you answered "Yes," which goal would you like to work on this week?_____

What **Action Steps** helped the most toward achieving your goal? _____

_____

Do you need to repeat any **Action Steps** to develop a habit?

_____

What did you notice and learn?_____

_____

WEEKLY RECAP – GRATITUDE:

Without looking back at what you have written down during the past week, answer the following questions:

What was the best part of your week?_____

_____

Who did you enjoy spending time with this week? _____

_____

Now look back at what you have written for the last week.

What do you notice about how you feel today versus how you felt in the moment? _____

_____

Did any of these moments contribute to your **Primary Goal**? If so, how? _____

_____

WEEKLY GOAL SETTING:

Refer to the previous page when completing this section.

If you did not meet your **Mini Goal**, what obstacles prevented you from doing so? _____

_____

_____

What **Action Steps** helped the most with your goal? Why?____

_____

_____

Do you need to repeat any **Action Steps** to help develop a habit? Which ones? _____

_____

What did you notice and learn?_____

_____

_____

My **Primary Goal** is: _____

The **Mini Goal** that I will work on this week is: _____

_____

Why is this **Mini Goal** important to your goal process?_____

_____

The habit that I would like to focus on to support my goal this week is: _____

Action Steps that I can do to work toward my goal this week are:

_____   _____

_____   _____

_____   _____

Plan out and list your **Action Steps** *and habit goals on the line for each day on the following page. As you complete these tasks, check them off!*

NEW WEEK + NEW FOCUS = NEW YOU:

My **Primary Goal** is: _____

It is important that I reach this goal because: _____

_____

_____

Each day list three things that make you feel grateful.

MONTH / DAY	1 _____
	2 _____
	3 _____

Action Step _____ Complete ❏

Habit goal _____ Complete ❏

Notes _____

MONTH / DAY	1 _____
	2 _____
	3 _____

Action Step _____ Complete ❏

Habit goal _____ Complete ❏

Notes _____

MONTH / DAY	1 _____
	2 _____
	3 _____

Action Step _____ Complete ❏

Habit goal _____ Complete ❏

Notes _____

MONTH / DAY	1 _____
	2 _____
	3 _____

Action Step _____ Complete ❏

Habit goal _____ Complete ❏

Notes _____

MONTH / DAY	1 _____
	2 _____
	3 _____

Action Step _____ Complete ❏

Habit goal _____ Complete ❏

Notes _____

MONTH / DAY	1 _____
	2 _____
	3 _____

Action Step _____ Complete ❏

Habit goal _____ Complete ❏

Notes _____

MONTH / DAY	1 _____
	2 _____
	3 _____

Action Step _____ Complete ❏

Habit goal _____ Complete ❏

Notes _____

WEEKLY RECAP – GOALS:

Did you meet your **Mini Goal** for this week? ❏ Yes ❏ No

If no, do you need to spend another week on this **Mini Goal** or would you prefer to move onto a new **Mini Goal** and return to this **Mini Goal** another time? ❏ Same ❏ New

If you answered "Yes," which goal would you like to work on this week?_____

What **Action Steps** helped the most toward achieving your goal? _____

_____

Do you need to repeat any **Action Steps** to develop a habit?

_____

What did you notice and learn?_____

_____

WEEKLY RECAP – GRATITUDE:

Without looking back at what you have written down during the past week, answer the following questions:

What was the best part of your week?_____

_____

Who did you enjoy spending time with this week? _____

_____

Now look back at what you have written for the last week.

What do you notice about how you feel today versus how you felt in the moment? _____

_____

Did any of these moments contribute to your **Primary Goal**? If so, how? _____

_____

WEEKLY GOAL SETTING:

Refer to the previous page when completing this section.

If you did not meet your **Mini Goal**, what obstacles prevented you from doing so? _____

_____

_____

What **Action Steps** helped the most with your goal? Why?____

_____

_____

Do you need to repeat any **Action Steps** to help develop a habit? Which ones? _____

_____

What did you notice and learn?_____

_____

_____

My **Primary Goal** is: _____

The **Mini Goal** that I will work on this week is: _____

_____

Why is this **Mini Goal** important to your goal process?_____

_____

The habit that I would like to focus on to support my goal this week is: _____

Action Steps that I can do to work toward my goal this week are:

_____   _____

_____   _____

_____   _____

Plan out and list your **Action Steps** *and habit goals on the line for each day on the following page. As you complete these tasks, check them off!*

NEW WEEK + NEW FOCUS = NEW YOU:

My **Primary Goal** is: _____

It is important that I reach this goal because: _____

_____

_____

Each day list three things that make you feel grateful.

MONTH / DAY	1 _____
	2 _____
	3 _____

Action Step _____ Complete ❏

Habit goal _____ Complete ❏

Notes _____

MONTH / DAY	1 _____
	2 _____
	3 _____

Action Step _____ Complete ❏

Habit goal _____ Complete ❏

Notes _____

MONTH / DAY	1 _____
	2 _____
	3 _____

Action Step _____ Complete ❏

Habit goal _____ Complete ❏

Notes _____

```
┌─────────┐
│ MONTH  ╱│   1 _____
│      ╱  │   2 _____
│    ╱    │   3 _____
│  ╱  DAY │
└─────────┘
```

Action Step _____ Complete ❏

Habit goal   _____ Complete ❏

Notes _____

```
┌─────────┐
│ MONTH  ╱│   1 _____
│      ╱  │   2 _____
│    ╱    │   3 _____
│  ╱  DAY │
└─────────┘
```

Action Step _____ Complete ❏

Habit goal   _____ Complete ❏

Notes _____

```
┌─────────┐
│ MONTH  ╱│   1 _____
│      ╱  │   2 _____
│    ╱    │   3 _____
│  ╱  DAY │
└─────────┘
```

Action Step _____ Complete ❏

Habit goal   _____ Complete ❏

Notes _____

```
┌─────────┐
│ MONTH  ╱│   1 _____
│      ╱  │   2 _____
│    ╱    │   3 _____
│  ╱  DAY │
└─────────┘
```

Action Step _____ Complete ❏

Habit goal   _____ Complete ❏

Notes _____

WEEKLY RECAP – GOALS:

Did you meet your **Mini Goal** for this week? ❑ Yes ❑ No

If no, do you need to spend another week on this **Mini Goal** or would you prefer to move onto a new **Mini Goal** and return to this **Mini Goal** another time? ❑ Same ❑ New

If you answered "Yes," which goal would you like to work on this week?_____

What **Action Steps** helped the most toward achieving your goal? _____

_____

Do you need to repeat any **Action Steps** to develop a habit?

_____

What did you notice and learn?_____

_____

WEEKLY RECAP – GRATITUDE:

Without looking back at what you have written down during the past week, answer the following questions:

What was the best part of your week?_____

_____

Who did you enjoy spending time with this week? _____

_____

Now look back at what you have written for the last week. What do you notice about how you feel today versus how you felt in the moment? _____

_____

Did any of these moments contribute to your **Primary Goal**? If so, how? _____

_____

WEEKLY GOAL SETTING:

Refer to the previous page when completing this section.
If you did not meet your **Mini Goal**, what obstacles prevented you from doing so? _____

_____

_____

What **Action Steps** helped the most with your goal? Why?____

_____

_____

Do you need to repeat any **Action Steps** to help develop a habit? Which ones? _____

_____

What did you notice and learn?_____

_____

_____

My **Primary Goal** is: _____

The **Mini Goal** that I will work on this week is: _____

_____

Why is this **Mini Goal** important to your goal process?_____

_____

The habit that I would like to focus on to support my goal this week is: _____

Action Steps that I can do to work toward my goal this week are:

_____   _____

_____   _____

_____   _____

Plan out and list your **Action Steps** *and habit goals on the line for each day on the following page. As you complete these tasks, check them off!*

NEW WEEK + NEW FOCUS = NEW YOU:

My **Primary Goal** is: _____

It is important that I reach this goal because: _____

_____

_____

Each day list three things that make you feel grateful.

MONTH / DAY	1 _____
	2 _____
	3 _____

Action Step _____ Complete ❏

Habit goal _____ Complete ❏

Notes _____

MONTH / DAY	1 _____
	2 _____
	3 _____

Action Step _____ Complete ❏

Habit goal _____ Complete ❏

Notes _____

MONTH / DAY	1 _____
	2 _____
	3 _____

Action Step _____ Complete ❏

Habit goal _____ Complete ❏

Notes _____

MONTH / DAY	1 _____
	2 _____
	3 _____

Action Step _____ Complete ❑

Habit goal _____ Complete ❑

Notes _____

MONTH / DAY	1 _____
	2 _____
	3 _____

Action Step _____ Complete ❑

Habit goal _____ Complete ❑

Notes _____

MONTH / DAY	1 _____
	2 _____
	3 _____

Action Step _____ Complete ❑

Habit goal _____ Complete ❑

Notes _____

MONTH / DAY	1 _____
	2 _____
	3 _____

Action Step _____ Complete ❑

Habit goal _____ Complete ❑

Notes _____

WEEKLY RECAP – GOALS:

Did you meet your **Mini Goal** for this week? ❏ Yes ❏ No
If no, do you need to spend another week on this **Mini Goal**
or would you prefer to move onto a new **Mini Goal** and return
to this **Mini Goal** another time? ❏ Same ❏ New
If you answered "Yes," which goal would you like to work on
this week?_____
What **Action Steps** helped the most toward achieving your
goal? _____
_____
Do you need to repeat any **Action Steps** to develop a habit?
_____
What did you notice and learn?_____

WEEKLY RECAP – GRATITUDE:

Without looking back at what you have written down during
the past week, answer the following questions:
What was the best part of your week?_____
_____
Who did you enjoy spending time with this week? _____
_____
Now look back at what you have written for the last week.
What do you notice about how you feel today versus how you
felt in the moment? _____
_____
Did any of these moments contribute to your **Primary Goal**? If
so, how? _____
_____

WEEKLY GOAL SETTING:

Refer to the previous page when completing this section.
If you did not meet your **Mini Goal**, what obstacles prevented you from doing so? _____

_____

_____

What **Action Steps** helped the most with your goal? Why?____

_____

_____

Do you need to repeat any **Action Steps** to help develop a habit? Which ones? _____

_____

What did you notice and learn?_____

_____

_____

My **Primary Goal** is: _____

The **Mini Goal** that I will work on this week is: _____

_____

Why is this **Mini Goal** important to your goal process?_____

_____

The habit that I would like to focus on to support my goal this week is: _____

Action Steps that I can do to work toward my goal this week are:

_____   _____

_____   _____

_____   _____

Plan out and list your **Action Steps** *and habit goals on the line for each day on the following page. As you complete these tasks, check them off!*

NEW WEEK + NEW FOCUS = NEW YOU:

My **Primary Goal** is: _____

It is important that I reach this goal because: _____

_____

_____

Each day list three things that make you feel grateful.

MONTH / DAY	
1	_____
2	_____
3	_____

Action Step _____ Complete ❏

Habit goal _____ Complete ❏

Notes _____

MONTH / DAY	
1	_____
2	_____
3	_____

Action Step _____ Complete ❏

Habit goal _____ Complete ❏

Notes _____

MONTH / DAY	
1	_____
2	_____
3	_____

Action Step _____ Complete ❏

Habit goal _____ Complete ❏

Notes _____

MONTH / DAY	1 _____
	2 _____
	3 _____

Action Step _____ Complete ❑

Habit goal _____ Complete ❑

Notes _____

MONTH / DAY	1 _____
	2 _____
	3 _____

Action Step _____ Complete ❑

Habit goal _____ Complete ❑

Notes _____

MONTH / DAY	1 _____
	2 _____
	3 _____

Action Step _____ Complete ❑

Habit goal _____ Complete ❑

Notes _____

MONTH / DAY	1 _____
	2 _____
	3 _____

Action Step _____ Complete ❑

Habit goal _____ Complete ❑

Notes _____

WEEKLY RECAP – GOALS:

Did you meet your **Mini Goal** for this week? ❑ Yes ❑ No
If no, do you need to spend another week on this **Mini Goal**
or would you prefer to move onto a new **Mini Goal** and return
to this **Mini Goal** another time? ❑ Same ❑ New
If you answered "Yes," which goal would you like to work on
this week?_____
What **Action Steps** helped the most toward achieving your
goal? _____
_____
Do you need to repeat any **Action Steps** to develop a habit?
_____
What did you notice and learn?_____
_____

WEEKLY RECAP – GRATITUDE:

Without looking back at what you have written down during
the past week, answer the following questions:
What was the best part of your week?_____
_____
Who did you enjoy spending time with this week? _____
_____
Now look back at what you have written for the last week.
What do you notice about how you feel today versus how you
felt in the moment? _____
_____
Did any of these moments contribute to your **Primary Goal**? If
so, how? _____
_____

WEEKLY GOAL SETTING:

Refer to the previous page when completing this section.

If you did not meet your **Mini Goal**, what obstacles prevented you from doing so? _____

_____

_____

What **Action Steps** helped the most with your goal? Why?____

_____

_____

Do you need to repeat any **Action Steps** to help develop a habit? Which ones? _____

_____

What did you notice and learn?_____

_____

_____

My **Primary Goal** is: _____

The **Mini Goal** that I will work on this week is: _____

_____

Why is this **Mini Goal** important to your goal process?_____

_____

The habit that I would like to focus on to support my goal this week is: _____

Action Steps that I can do to work toward my goal this week are:

_____   _____

_____   _____

_____   _____

Plan out and list your **Action Steps** *and habit goals on the line for each day on the following page. As you complete these tasks, check them off!*

NEW WEEK + NEW FOCUS = NEW YOU:

My **Primary Goal** is: _____

It is important that I reach this goal because: _____

_____

_____

Each day list three things that make you feel grateful.

```
┌─────────┐   1 _____
│ MONTH ╱ │
│      ╱  │   2 _____
│    ╱    │
│  ╱  DAY │   3 _____
└─────────┘
```

Action Step _____ Complete ❏

Habit goal   _____ Complete ❏

Notes _____

```
┌─────────┐   1 _____
│ MONTH ╱ │
│      ╱  │   2 _____
│    ╱    │
│  ╱  DAY │   3 _____
└─────────┘
```

Action Step _____ Complete ❏

Habit goal   _____ Complete ❏

Notes _____

```
┌─────────┐   1 _____
│ MONTH ╱ │
│      ╱  │   2 _____
│    ╱    │
│  ╱  DAY │   3 _____
└─────────┘
```

Action Step _____ Complete ❏

Habit goal   _____ Complete ❏

Notes _____

```
┌─────────┐
│ MONTH  ╱│   1 _____
│      ╱  │   2 _____
│    ╱ DAY│   3 _____
└─────────┘
```

Action Step _____ Complete ❏

Habit goal _____ Complete ❏

Notes _____

```
┌─────────┐
│ MONTH  ╱│   1 _____
│      ╱  │   2 _____
│    ╱ DAY│   3 _____
└─────────┘
```

Action Step _____ Complete ❏

Habit goal _____ Complete ❏

Notes _____

```
┌─────────┐
│ MONTH  ╱│   1 _____
│      ╱  │   2 _____
│    ╱ DAY│   3 _____
└─────────┘
```

Action Step _____ Complete ❏

Habit goal _____ Complete ❏

Notes _____

```
┌─────────┐
│ MONTH  ╱│   1 _____
│      ╱  │   2 _____
│    ╱ DAY│   3 _____
└─────────┘
```

Action Step _____ Complete ❏

Habit goal _____ Complete ❏

Notes _____

WEEKLY RECAP – GOALS:

Did you meet your **Mini Goal** for this week? ❑ Yes ❑ No
If no, do you need to spend another week on this **Mini Goal**
or would you prefer to move onto a new **Mini Goal** and return
to this **Mini Goal** another time? ❑ Same ❑ New
If you answered "Yes," which goal would you like to work on
this week?_____
What **Action Steps** helped the most toward achieving your
goal? _____
_____
Do you need to repeat any **Action Steps** to develop a habit?
_____
What did you notice and learn?_____
_____

WEEKLY RECAP – GRATITUDE:

Without looking back at what you have written down during
the past week, answer the following questions:
What was the best part of your week?_____
_____
Who did you enjoy spending time with this week? _____
_____
Now look back at what you have written for the last week.
What do you notice about how you feel today versus how you
felt in the moment? _____
_____
Did any of these moments contribute to your **Primary Goal**? If
so, how? _____
_____

WEEKLY GOAL SETTING:

Refer to the previous page when completing this section.

If you did not meet your **Mini Goal**, what obstacles prevented you from doing so? _____

_____

_____

What **Action Steps** helped the most with your goal? Why?____

_____

_____

Do you need to repeat any **Action Steps** to help develop a habit? Which ones? _____

_____

What did you notice and learn?_____

_____

_____

My **Primary Goal** is: _____

The **Mini Goal** that I will work on this week is: _____

_____

Why is this **Mini Goal** important to your goal process?_____

_____

The habit that I would like to focus on to support my goal this week is: _____

Action Steps that I can do to work toward my goal this week are:

_____   _____

_____   _____

_____   _____

*Plan out and list your **Action Steps** and habit goals on the line for each day on the following page. As you complete these tasks, check them off!*

NEW WEEK + NEW FOCUS = NEW YOU:

My **Primary Goal** is: _____

It is important that I reach this goal because: _____

_____

_____

Each day list three things that make you feel grateful.

```
MONTH
          DAY
```
1 _____
2 _____
3 _____

Action Step _____ Complete ❏

Habit goal _____ Complete ❏

Notes _____

```
MONTH
          DAY
```
1 _____
2 _____
3 _____

Action Step _____ Complete ❏

Habit goal _____ Complete ❏

Notes _____

```
MONTH
          DAY
```
1 _____
2 _____
3 _____

Action Step _____ Complete ❏

Habit goal _____ Complete ❏

Notes _____

```
┌─────────┐
│ MONTH  ╱│   1 _____
│      ╱  │   2 _____
│    ╱    │   3 _____
│  ╱  DAY │
└─────────┘
```

Action Step _____ Complete ❏

Habit goal _____ Complete ❏

Notes _____

```
┌─────────┐
│ MONTH  ╱│   1 _____
│      ╱  │   2 _____
│    ╱    │   3 _____
│  ╱  DAY │
└─────────┘
```

Action Step _____ Complete ❏

Habit goal _____ Complete ❏

Notes _____

```
┌─────────┐
│ MONTH  ╱│   1 _____
│      ╱  │   2 _____
│    ╱    │   3 _____
│  ╱  DAY │
└─────────┘
```

Action Step _____ Complete ❏

Habit goal _____ Complete ❏

Notes _____

```
┌─────────┐
│ MONTH  ╱│   1 _____
│      ╱  │   2 _____
│    ╱    │   3 _____
│  ╱  DAY │
└─────────┘
```

Action Step _____ Complete ❏

Habit goal _____ Complete ❏

Notes _____

WEEKLY RECAP – GOALS:

Did you meet your **Mini Goal** for this week? ❑ Yes ❑ No

If no, do you need to spend another week on this **Mini Goal** or would you prefer to move onto a new **Mini Goal** and return to this **Mini Goal** another time? ❑ Same ❑ New

If you answered "Yes," which goal would you like to work on this week?_____

What **Action Steps** helped the most toward achieving your goal? _____

_____

Do you need to repeat any **Action Steps** to develop a habit?

_____

What did you notice and learn?_____

_____

WEEKLY RECAP – GRATITUDE:

Without looking back at what you have written down during the past week, answer the following questions:

What was the best part of your week?_____

_____

Who did you enjoy spending time with this week? _____

_____

Now look back at what you have written for the last week. What do you notice about how you feel today versus how you felt in the moment? _____

_____

Did any of these moments contribute to your **Primary Goal**? If so, how? _____

_____

WEEKLY GOAL SETTING:

Refer to the previous page when completing this section.
If you did not meet your **Mini Goal**, what obstacles prevented you from doing so? _____

_____
_____

What **Action Steps** helped the most with your goal? Why?____

_____
_____

Do you need to repeat any **Action Steps** to help develop a habit? Which ones? _____

_____

What did you notice and learn?_____

_____
_____

My **Primary Goal** is: _____
The **Mini Goal** that I will work on this week is: _____

_____

Why is this **Mini Goal** important to your goal process?_____

_____

The habit that I would like to focus on to support my goal this week is: _____

Action Steps that I can do to work toward my goal this week are:

_____   _____

_____   _____

_____   _____

*Plan out and list your **Action Steps** and habit goals on the line for each day on the following page. As you complete these tasks, check them off!*

Here you are at the end of the workbook!

You made it! You're awesome! Take a minute to ponder your journey.

What was your greatest achievement in this process?_____
_____
_____
_____

What challenged you the most and why? _____
_____
_____
_____

What did you notice after you began tracking your gratitude regularly? _____
_____
_____

Was there a point in the process where you wanted to quit but you kept going? If so, what kept you going?_____
_____
_____
_____

Are you ready to tackle your next goal? If you need more time to dedicate to this goal, order another copy of the *Goals with Gratitude Workbook,* and also consider gifting one to someone special.